Joyful Mother Of Children

TOYIN ADEWUNMI

EMMANUEL HOUSE
London, United Kingdom

Joyful Mother of Children
Copyright © 2002 by Toyin Adewunmi

Published by
Emmanuel House
PO Box 15022
London SE5 7ZL
United Kingdom
Info@emmanuel-house.org.uk

All Scriptures, unless otherwise stated, are from the Holy Bible, *New International Version*. Copyright © 1973, 1978, 1984 by International Bible Society. Used by permission.

All rights reserved. No part of this publication may be reproduced, stored in a retrieval system, or be transmitted in any form or by any means, mechanical, electronic, photocopying or otherwise without the prior written consent of the copyright owner.

ISBN 1 900529 17 3

Cover Design by *Efih*
Printed in England by Omnia Books Ltd.

Contents

Acknowledgements
Dedication
Foreword
Introduction   **11**

1. I Loved Children   **17**
2. Out of the Miry Clay   **23**
3. What is the Lord Requiring of You?   **35**
4. Confronted by the Enemy   **43**
5. Don't Crack the Wall   **47**
6. Whose Report Will You Believe?   **57**
7. Be Quiet   **65**
8. The Humiliation   **75**
9. I Thought God Was in it   **81**
10. Only Christ Can Comfort You   **93**
11. Remember Me, Oh Lord!   **99**
12. How Could This Be?   **105**
13. My Deliverance From "Aota" Spirit   **113**
14. Spiritual Husbandry   **117**
15. Break the Legal Ground of Curses   **121**
16. And the Lord Remembered Me!   **125**
17. He is Never Too Late   **133**
18. Abraham and Sarah   **141**
19. He Will do it Again!   **153**

Acknowledgements

Firstly, my words of appreciation and thanksgiving goes to the *Alpha*, the Lord of the whole universe Who has qualified me to be a partaker of the inheritance of the saints in the light. He has delivered me from the power of darkness and translated me into the Kingdom of the Son of His love - Our Lord Jesus Christ, in whom I have redemption through His blood, the forgiveness of sins.

My sincere thanks also goes to Kayode Adewumi and Gbenga Badejo. I appreciate your support in proofing this book several times.

My words of gratitude also goes to Rev. Timothy Kolade (National Overseer NCC, United Kingdom). Thank you sir for your support. I also appreciate your humility to write the foreword to this book. May the good Lord reward you and crown your undertakings with success.

I acknowledge Rev. Mrs Kate Jinadu. Thank you ma, for your encouragements and being there for me always. You are a mother indeed.

To our lovely children. Thank you for bearing with me throughout the time of writing this book. May God bless you and make His face to continually shine upon you. May He reward your patience and understanding.

To Tokunbo Emmanuel, my publisher, who gladly accepted to publish this book. Thank you so much for your editorial input and reassuring words.

Thank you to my parents for bringing me up in the way of the Lord, for your patience and love. I appreciate and love you both with my whole heart.

To my husband Gbenro, my mentor and my crown. I appreciate you for your kindness, gentleness and simplicity. Thank you for releasing me into what God has called me to do, for your encouragement and support. I do celebrate you. I also want you to know how valuable you are to me. Blessed are you for the love you have loved me with. Thank you for sticking by me through the difficult times. We have been through so many tough situations together and the Lord has helped again and again to overcome them.

Lastly, to the *Omega*, my Lord Jesus Christ, who has counted me worthy of this call. A good God at all time, a perfect God at all time. You do not need to improve on Your character. You do not need to graduate from good to better then best. You are forever the same. To say You are the "best" God is inaccurate; the truth is this, You are the *only* God. Nothing and no-one can be compared with You. To You be the glory and dominion and power forever and ever, Amen. Thank you for being there for me when all else failed. Knowing you is a privilege, serving you is an opportunity.

To the glory of the Almighty God, this book is dedicated to my lovely children. You are indeed God's blessing to me and you are my testimony. May you continue to be God's blessing to us your parents, to the body of Christ and to your generation.

This book is also dedicated to everyone trusting God for the fruit of the womb. As the Lord took me by the hand, led me out of the difficult situation, may He also take you by the hand and lead you to absolute fruitfulness.

Foreword

This book is a clear testimony of the tangible power of God intervening in human affairs. As stated in Hebrews 4:12, you are soon to discover that God's word truly pierces into the fabric of the human anatomy.

> **the word of God is living and powerful and sharper than any two-edged sword, piercing even to the division of soul and spirit and of joints and marrow, and is a discerner of the thoughts and intents of the heart.**

Toyin writes from every position of advantage, not only about what she has heard or seen, but also what her hands have handled of the word of life. She is not ashamed to expose her weaknesses and reveal how God strengthened her throughout her quest for a child. There is no argument that can deny personal experience because many of the things that shake us do, eventually, shape us.

Let this book provoke your faith and expose any barrenness in your life to God's fruitfulness. By presenting her testimony in a simple form, Toyin has made it possible for you to taste and experience the benefit of seeing God turn your impotence around by His omnipotence. I am sure you will have a testimony.

- Rev. Timothy Kolade
National Overseer
New Covenant Church, UK

Introduction

God revealed plans about this book to me four and a half years after telling me that He would use me to minister to those trusting God for the fruit of the womb. At that time, I was planning to start a business. I had gone to the Lord in prayer for a name for the business and for direction as to where to locate. Although I was working as a nurse, I had a desire to set up my own business. It was after I had made these requests that the Lord spoke to me.

God made me realise that He had something more important in mind than what I was asking. He was concerned about the afflictions of His people tormented with childlessness. The problem was even heavier on His heart than in the hearts of those going through it. He wanted people to be released from this bondage because He had not ordained barrenness in the life of any woman.

Before this revelation and while still unmarried, I had a burden for women who were finding it difficult to bear children. The burden became so heavy on my heart that I had to set apart a day each week to fast and pray for them without their knowledge. To the glory of God, many of them are now with children.

There was a particular woman who had a prime place in my heart during the time I was trusting God for our children. When I heard her story, I was so moved that I started to pray for God to answer her before me. I want to thank the Lord for honouring the prayer. She now has a boy.

I had fertility problems after I got married due to several things that happened to me before I became a Christian. All these I have unveiled in this book, including how the Lord brought me out of the mess I was in.

There is nothing new under heaven. History always repeats itself. You will save yourself a lot of heartache learning from what I went through. Whoever takes time to learn from other people's mistakes is wise. King Solomon related this truth to us in Ecclesiastes.

> **What has been will be again, what has been done will be done again; there is nothing new under the sun. Is there anything of which one can say, "Look! This is something new"? It was here already, long ago; it was here before our time (Ecclesiastes 1:9-10).**

YOUR "JOURNEY PLANNER"

In 1994, a year after I got married, the Lord showed up in my dream. He told me that I was in Satan's

Introduction

bondage and that He will deliver me in the church I was attending (of which I am still a member). He mentioned the name of our General Overseer and promised that He will use him to deliver me. The Lord also told me that when I am set free, He would use me to minister to others in the same predicament. God knows the end from the beginning. I did not know how He was going to do it and in what capacity he would be using me until He told me to write this book.

When the Lord spoke to me about the solution to my problem, I thought it would vanish in a moment, and I will start having children immediately. I was wrong. In fact, that was just the beginning of the whole journey. Thanks be to the Lord who armed me with strength throughout my waiting period. He made my feet like the deer's; He set me on my high places and He taught my hands to make war.

This book is not just about my season of infertility, things that led to it and how the Lord got me out of it; it is a book that will minister to the needs of people with fertility problems. My prayer is that as you read along, the Lord will unveil to you deep secrets about your own life and situation. He will walk with you through your passage of fear into a place of absolute rest in Him. God will find you out and help you receive solutions to your problems.

Trusting God for a child, I believe, is a journey that you cannot embark upon on your own. You need God's direction as your "journey planner" which will keep you focused and will prevent you from being tossed about. It will also prevent you from fighting as someone beating the air or going round in circles.

When the Lord gave me my "journey planner" (and told me how the yoke of barrenness would be broken in my life), I did not recognise it. I lost focus of what the Lord had said because I lacked understanding. How can one focus on something that is not acknowledged or recognised?

Abraham received a "journey planner" for his own situation but he, also, did not keep his focus on the word of God.

> After this, the word of the LORD came to Abram in a vision: "Do not be afraid, Abram. I am your shield, your very great reward." But Abram said, "O Sovereign LORD, what can you give me since I remain childless and the one who will inherit my estate is Eliezer of Damascus?" And Abram said, "You have given me no children; so a servant in my household will be my heir." Then the word of the LORD came to him: "This man will not be your heir, but a son coming from your own body will be your heir." He took him outside and said, "Look up at the heavens and count the stars—if indeed you can count them." Then he said to him, "So shall your offspring be." Abram believed the LORD, and he credited it to him as righteousness (Gen. 15:1-6).

He yielded to Sarah's suggestion to go in to Hagar and that remains a problem up till today (I will discuss the story of Abraham in chapter 18). It is not enough to receive a "journey planner" from God; one needs to recognise, understand, and follow it. You need to keep your focus. Hannah received a "journey planner" from the Lord, followed it and received her blessing. (Read about Hannah in chapter 3).

God is faithful. He will provide you with a personal "journey planner" that leads to fruitfulness. Allow God to open your spiritual eyes to see and tap into this necessary resource. Keep an open mind always to what God says to you. If you are not sure of what He is saying, go back to Him and ask. If you do not receive direction from God, it does not mean that you would not receive your hearts desire eventually. However, receiving and recognising God's plan for the situation can save you a lot of trouble, heartache, time and unnecessary mistakes.

Whatever the Lord may minister to you as you read this book, act on them and you will be glad you did. Remember, He knows the end from the beginning.

CHAPTER 1

I Loved Children

The midday sun was shinning at its brightest on this beautiful day. I was in a hurry to reach my destination. I began to run down the road, not giving any attention to the heavy sweat that was drenching my clothes. Moments later, I noticed some children were running after me. Scared that they would hinder my progress, I increased my strides, not wanting any of them to touch me. Eventually, I saw a house and ran into it. One of the children entered the house with me. My heart began to accelerate faster than ever. I could feel the pounding like the vibrations of a big bass drum.

My heart was still pounding when I woke up from sleep. What a relief, it was just a dream!

I used to have negative ideas about having children and I grew up with these wrong beliefs. Convinced that childbearing would hinder my progress in life, my mind was made up: I would not have children until I reached a certain stage in my career, regardless of my age.

After I gave my life to Christ I began to view children from a different perspective. I developed a fondness for children and was eager to have children of my own soon after marriage.

Out of this interest in children with a desire to bring them up in the way of the Lord, I enrolled for a course on Children Evangelism in 1992. I learnt how to lead children to Christ and how to teach them the way of the Lord. This acquired knowledge further increased my excitement about having children. I had no recollection of the negative things I had said and thought about childbearing.

When I first discovered in 1993 that I was not conceiving, fear gripped me. The spiritual preparation I had gone through – the Children Evangelism course – had raised my hopes about bringing up my own children. I dreaded the cutting short of my expectations. I did not want my hope to die just there.

My fears escalated when I recalled the several negative prophesies people had spoken against my future in the *white garment* church I attended when growing up. Troubled by haunting memories and uncertain hope, I prayed, fasted and sought the Lord's face for a child, but nothing happened. Several times, I went for deliverance prayer sessions without any good result. It was as if the heavens were shut against me.

I soon realised that there was a limit to human ability and understanding. The harder I tried to make conception take place, the more I discovered the bitter truth that I could not help myself. I read extensively on infertility — its causes and the medical treatments available. But, the more I read, the more I discovered that I needed God's intervention.

After what seemed like endless months of trying, I finally decided to leave everything in God's hands. I submitted to God agreeing not to rely on my own knowledge and understanding any longer.

Trust in the Lord with all your heart and lean not on your own understanding, in all your ways acknowledge Him and He shall direct your paths (Proverbs 3:5,6).

In your desire to bear children, have you reached this point yet? Have you made the discovery that only God can make the difference? I know the pain that accompanies childlessness, but through it all, depend wholly on the Lord. He cannot mislead you. He knows everything that concerns you. He knows the end of what you are going through even before you found yourself in the circumstance. The medical knowledge you possess regarding your situation is great, but know that God's understanding and wisdom surpasses human knowledge.

> Do you not know? Have you not heard? The LORD is the everlasting God, the Creator of the ends of the earth. He will not grow tired or weary, and His understanding no one can fathom (Isaiah 40:28).

> Great is our Lord and mighty in power; His understanding has no limit (Psalm 147:5).

BATTLES IN THE NIGHT

God is the only one who has the key and solution to the problem of infertility. In spite of the battles we may experience, we know that God has secured the ultimate victory.

When I became aware of my need for God's intervention in my condition, the devil started to oppress me in my dreams. The oppression was so much that I often dreaded lying on the bed in case I fell asleep. I usually went to bed hoping to keep my eyes open throughout the night. After struggling with my tired eyelids, I would, each time, drift off to sleep.

During these night battles, I learnt about God's graciousness in helping us to sleep and waking us up each morning. He was always faithful to His words even when I was afraid to close my eyes.

> I lay down and I slept; I awoke for the Lord sustained me (Psalm 3:5, NKJV).

> I will both lie down in peace and sleep, for you alone O Lord make me dwell in safety (Psalm 4:8).

These Psalms were written by David when his enemies oppressed him intensely. The afflictions I endured were also very fierce that I once had to ask the Lord, in my dream, for the reason why He allowed the devil to torment me that much. His reply was revealing. God told me that 'He needs someone who will be able to withstand the test of time; someone He could give the great task of ministering to those waiting on God for the fruit of the womb.' He also said that 'He needs someone He will try and find to be faithful and true.'

God gave me the grace to endure Satan's attacks. He taught me a lot through the battles I encountered. At the end of it all, I found out that God is dependable. His plans will always stand sure. His words are forever settled in heaven. Remember always, therefore, that God's original intention for mankind is fruitfulness and multiplication. This is His purpose for you too—no matter the difficulties you go through.

So God created man in His own image; in the image of God He created him; male and female He created them. Then God blessed them and said to them, *be fruitful and multiply;* **fill the earth and subdue it. Rule over the fish of the sea and the birds of the air and over every living creature that moves on the ground. (Genesis 1:27,28,** *Italics mine***).**

The blessing of fruitfulness is the first blessing God pronounced on mankind. This shows how important reproduction is to God. The Lord always keeps watch over His words to bring them to fulfilment (Jeremiah 1:12). Whatever forces are working against the blessing that God proclaimed on mankind must bow to the power of the Holy Spirit. By the grace of God, I have unveiled many of these wicked forces in this book. As you read on, you will discover the truth and experience freedom.

CHAPTER 2

Out Of The Miry Clay

I grew up in one of the *white garment* churches in Nigeria. I attended the church for eighteen years. Worship in this church (and churches of its kind) involved all sorts of occult practices. Many evil practices were concealed under the frequent ceremonies. Most people attending these churches are unaware of what actually transpires.

I went through all sorts of prayer rituals while a member. Innocently, I considered myself a good, prayerful Christian, when in actual fact, I was communing with fallen angels. Many of the so-called prophets had obtained their powers and prophetic gifts from fetish doctors. I lived, for many years, under religious deception.

NEGATIVE PROPHECIES

The words of 'prophecy' from the prophets in this *white garment* church brought terror and calamity upon the lives of members. I was told that I would never be able to bear children. This word was spoken over me a couple of times by different 'prophets.' I was not really worried about the thought of living without children of my own. As I wrote earlier, at the time I considered children a hindrance. I was not at all perturbed. It actually strengthened my resolve not to have anything to do with children. My senior sister, however, was concerned.

When these prophets of doom prophesied, it could be that they were actually seeing the future, howbeit, through the power of the devil. These prophets are likened to the prophets described by Jeremiah in the Bible. Whatever they prophesied was activated and brought to manifestation by demonic spirits.

> I have heard what the prophets say who prophesy lies in my name. They say, 'I had a dream! I had a dream!' How long will this continue in the hearts of these lying prophets, who prophesy the delusions of their own minds? They think the dreams they tell one another will make my people forget my name, just as their fathers forgot my name through Baal worship. Let the prophet who has a dream tell his dream, but let the one who has my word speak it faithfully. For what has straw to do with grain?" declares the LORD. "Is not my word like fire," declares the LORD, "and like a hammer that breaks a rock in pieces? "Therefore," declares the LORD, "I am against the prophets who steal from one another words supposedly from me. Yes," declares the LORD, "I am against the prophets who wag their own tongues and yet declare,

> 'The LORD declares.' Indeed, I am against those who prophesy false dreams," declares the LORD. "They tell them and lead my people astray with their reckless lies, yet I did not send or appoint them. They do not benefit these people in the least," declares the LORD (Jeremiah 23:25-32).

These prophets prophesy lies and deceit to people in the name of God; people go astray as a result. They also cause people to abandon the true worship of God for demon worship. The bible describes them as chaff and the Lord says He is against such. Many people, I have observed, are in bondage to these mediums. Urged on by the need for solutions to their problems and blinded by ignorance, many run after 'prophets' and 'prophecies.'

If you visit occult houses in search for prophecies to end seasons of childlessness, know now that *white garment* prophets cannot profit you. They only increase calamity in the lives of innocent souls. Refrain from them.

TEST OF PROPHETS

The Bible has a lot to say about prophets and how to prove them.

> Dear friends, do not believe every spirit, but test the spirits to see whether they are from God, because many false prophets have gone out into the world. This is how you can recognize the Spirit of God: Every spirit that acknowledges that Jesus

> Christ has come in the flesh is from God, but every spirit that does not acknowledge Jesus is not from God. This is the spirit of the antichrist, which you have heard is coming and even now is already in the world (1 John 4:1-3).

> Two or three prophets should speak, and the others should weigh carefully what is said (1 Corinthians 14:29).

The Bible also teaches that the origin of all spiritual gifts is the Spirit of God. There is no short cut nor intermediaries. Moreover, these gifts are for the profit of all (unlike false "prophecies" that do not profit the recipients).

> There are different kinds of working, but the same God works all of them in all men. Now to each one the manifestation of the Spirit is given for the common good. To one there is given through the Spirit the message of wisdom, to another the message of knowledge by means of the same Spirit, to another faith by the same Spirit, to another gifts of healing by that one Spirit, to another miraculous powers, to another prophecy, to another distinguishing between spirits, to another speaking in different kinds of tongues, and to still another the interpretation of tongues. All these are the work of one and the same Spirit, and he gives them to each one, just as he determines (1 Corinthians 12:6-11).

WHAT SHOULD COME OUT OF PROPHECY?

But everyone who prophesies speaks to men for their strengthening, encouragement and comfort (1 Corinthians 14:3).

From the scriptural verse, a word of prophecy will bring three things into the life of recipients.

- *Edification or strengthening*: to build up in character or faith; improvement of the mind or morals.
- *Exhortation or encouragement*: to encourage, religious discourse.
- *Comfort*: to console, to allay grief or anxiety, to cheer, gladden.

Every true prophecy must be in line with the word of God and edify the saints. It must not bring fear upon the lives of people. Perhaps you have been through this kind of ordeal and wonder if there is help. Indeed, there is. The Scriptures declare in Proverbs 26:2,

Like a flitting sparrow, like a flying swallow, so a curse without cause shall not alight (NKJV).

People, in the guise of prophecy, may have said negative things concerning your ability to reproduce, but in the name of Jesus, these words shall not stand.

TIME TO LEAVE?

The Lord in His infinite mercies drew me out of the white garment church in a miraculous way. Before June 1991, I was adamant that nothing could draw me out of the church. Fear was the main factor behind my resolve.

Firstly, people who left the church were always seen as rebels and I did not want to be rebellious. Secondly, people who left the church were placed under curses; that they would get into serious difficulties after leaving the church, with problems that no one on this earth would be able to solve (in most cases, life-threatening diseases) until they returned to the church. Thirdly, we were taught to see non-members as inferior. In spirituality, we ranked next to God. Why should I leave a high place for a lower one?

The spiritual leaders were never worried when a member of the church left because they believed the person will soon come back begging. So, I never thought of leaving.

OVERPOWERED BY GOD'S LOVE; CAUGHT IN HIS NET

In spite of this fear, I attended several Christian gatherings and was personally ministered to on many occasions, but I did not make any commitment.

One day, I became thirsty for something but did not know what it was. I felt empty and wanted to be filled. This great longing went on within me for months. It was as if I had a desperate need in my life. I tried to meet the need but could not. Eventually, I began to search for Christian literatures I had received in the past. I could not explain why I chose to satisfy my thirst by reading Christian literature, but that was what I did.

The more I read, the more thirsty I became. So, I kept on reading. Even after reading the books over and over again, I was not entirely satisfied. I felt there was more to know. So I decided to read the Bible — which I had not read since I finished my secondary school certificate examination seven years before.

I received a copy of the Gideon's New Testament Bible in secondary school. It did not take too long to read from Matthew through to Revelation several times. The more I read, the deeper the yearning within my heart grew. There was an emptiness in my life that needed to be filled but I did not know how to fill it.

THE MISSING PART

During this period, I fell ill and a Christian friend came to visit me. She had told me about Jesus Christ several times in the past but the message had not registered in my heart. Of a truth, "no one can come to [God] unless the Father who sent [Jesus] draws him" (John 6:44).

This time, when my friend was about to leave, she called my name and said, "you need to give your life to Christ." Immediately, like a ray of light through thick darkness, it clicked that she had just mentioned my heart's desire. For months, I had been searching, not knowing that Jesus Christ was the missing part of my life.

My friend could not believe her ears when I asked her what I needed to do. She happily led me to Christ. Oh what a joy I felt! Jesus Christ was indeed the One my heart yearned for! All my thirst and hunger were satisfied in an instant. Jesus became my Saviour, Lord and Master. For the first time in my life, I read the Bible and understood it.

COME TO THE WATERS

If you are thirsty as I was, come to the waters of life, Jesus Christ. Drink of Him and you will thirst no more. He has been waiting for you with open arms. No one is too sinful to come to Him; no one is too bad. You do not need money to get through to Jesus. Just come as you are.

> **Come, all you who are thirsty, come to the waters; and you who have no money, come, buy and eat! Come, buy wine and milk without money and without cost. Why spend money on what is not bread, and your labour on what does not satisfy? Listen, listen to me, and eat what is good, and your soul will delight in the richest of fare (Isaiah 55:1-2).**

God gives His Spirit and Word to the hungry without price. Do not spend your life on what cannot satisfy or fill. Jesus is the real bread, the 'Bread of life'; eat of Him and let your soul delight in abundance.

I am the bread of life. Your forefathers ate the manna in the desert, yet they died. But here is the bread that comes down from heaven, which a man may eat and not die. I am the living bread that came down from heaven. If anyone eats of this bread, he will live forever. This bread is my flesh, which I will give for the life of the world (John 6:48-51).

Jesus Christ is the God that I now serve. He gave me a reason to live and a hope beyond this world. Even my latter desire for children did not compare with the joy of knowing Christ as my Saviour. I began to have a new hope that everything was going to be alright.

THE GREATEST NEED

You probably started reading this book because of your need for a child. Be rest assured, Jesus can and will make you a joyful mother of children. I must, however, help you fulfill a greater need, which is that of knowing Jesus as your Saviour.

If only for this life we have hope in Christ, we are to be pitied more than all men (1 Corinthians 15:19).

Are you prepared for life after death? Do you know where you will spend eternity? Take some time to think of these things. If you are uncertain of your future hope, the following will help you find peace with God through Jesus Christ.

Acknowledge that you are a sinner. There is a need to be sincere and honest about yourself. It does not matter what sins you have or have not committed. Everyone who has not received Christ Jesus as Lord and Saviour is a sinner.

For all have sinned and have fall short of the glory of God (Romans 3:23).

Confess your sins before Him. Go a step further by repentantly confessing your sins to God. He is ready to forgive and give you a new life.

If we claim to be without sin, we deceive ourselves and the truth is not in us. If we confess our sins, He is faithful and just and will forgive us our sins and purify us from all unrighteousness. If we claim we have not sinned, we make Him out to be a liar and His word has no place in our lives (1 John 1:8,9).

Confess and believe in Jesus. You also need to declare with your mouth that Jesus Christ is your Lord and Saviour, and believe in your heart that God raised Him from the dead for your sake.

> That if you confess with your mouth, "Jesus is Lord," and believe in your heart that God raised him from the dead, you will be saved. For it is with your heart that you believe and are justified, and it is with your mouth that you confess and are saved (Romans 10:9-10).

Find a Bible-believing Church to attend. At the point of salvation, you are just like a baby. You will need to surround yourself with people who are matured in the things of God; people who can encourage, motivate and challenge your Christian walk. You will need to be fed with the word of God in a good Church environment. A commitment to attend fellowship with other believers for the purpose of learning God's ways, prayer and communion is also essential.

> They devoted themselves to the apostles' teaching and to the fellowship, to the breaking of bread and to prayer (Acts 2:42).

I pray you find in Jesus the joy that I found when I gave my heart to Him. As I later discovered, knowing Jesus made all the difference in my yearning to give birth to a child of my own.

CHAPTER 3

What Is The Lord Requiring Of You?

About a year before I got married, I attended a programme organised by a Pentecostal church. In the middle of the service, I felt the Lord asking me to give all the money I had on me as a *seed* for my children. *How can I sow a seed for children I do not yet have?*, I wondered. Besides, I was not married.

All I had on me was the travel fare for a journey to see my parents. I decided to sow a third of the money as the seed and spend the rest on transportation. I realised much later that I had consumed my seed when I decided to spend two-thirds of what I was asked to give. I did not remember this incident again until I began to experience difficulties in conceiving. I then started sowing endlessly and desperately, even when the Lord did not ask me to, but nothing favourable resulted from my giving.

IT'S NOT A TIME FOR STORIES

We are privileged when God asks us to sow seeds, whether it is money, time, skills or any other thing. I now see sowing as an opportunity to harvest. You will discover that most of the things God specifically asks us to give, they are usually those things that mean a lot to us; small but precious things. Our lack of understanding could cause us to make excuses like the Samaritan woman at the well (John 4:1-26).

Jesus asked the Samaritan woman for a drink of water. In response, she started telling stories about how Jews and Samaritans do not relate with one another. She told Jesus who dug the well and the people that had drank from it. She did not realise that the 'River of Life' had given her the opportunity to be blessed. Thank God her eyes of understanding were opened before it was too late. She realised Jesus was able to give her something greater than the well she had been telling stories about.

What is the Lord requiring from you?

Hear, O my people, and I will speak, O Israel, and I will testify against you: I am God, your God. I do not rebuke you for your sacrifices or your burnt offerings, which are ever before me. I have no need of a bull from your stall or of goats from your pens, for every animal of the forest is mine, and the cattle on a thousand hills. I know every bird in the mountains, and the creatures of the field are mine. If I were hungry I would not tell you, for the world is mine, and all that is in it. (Psalm 50:7-12).

The earth belongs to the Lord and everything inside it, including *you*. If He was really hungry for the things He requires from us, He would help Himself without asking—and there is nothing anyone can do to prevent Him. God is all-sufficient. However, when He asks us to give, He wants us to do so cheerfully out of our free wills. This gives us the opportunity to be blessed.

ABRAHAM'S SACRIFICE

Abraham looked for an offspring with Sarah for 60 years. (In Hebrew culture, men usually get married at 40). Eventually, God gave them a son called Isaac. God later asked Abraham to sacrifice this precious child they had so much desired. Abraham did not argue with God, neither did he remind God of the promised child. Even Isaac did not struggle with his father. At the point of Abraham's obedience, God showed up. He gave Abraham a ram to sacrifice in place of his son. The Lord proclaimed His blessing upon Abraham as a result of his obedience and readiness to let go of everything that belonged to him, including Isaac. Abraham's blessing was four-fold and sealed with an oath:

The angel of the LORD called to Abraham from heaven a second time and said, "I swear by myself, declares the LORD, that because you have done this and have not withheld your son, your only son, I will surely bless you and make your descendants as numerous as the stars in the sky

and as the sand on the seashore. Your descendants will take possession of the cities of their enemies, and through your offspring all nations on earth will be blessed, because you have obeyed me" (Gen. 22:15-18).

He swore by Himself (1) to bless Abraham; (2) to make his descendants as numerous as the stars in the sky; (3) to give Abraham's descendants possession of the cities of their enemies; and (4) to bless all the nations of the earth through his offspring.

God often asks us for costly and dear things. When we take a bold step of faith to obey His voice as Abraham did, He will surely bless us. We can sing "Abraham's blessings are mine," but if he had not obeyed God's voice, the song will be meaningless today. This goes to show that when we obey God, it is not only the person involved that gets blessed, but other people as well, including our children. On the other hand, when we disobey, people around us are also adversely affected.

God at times asks for things that seem senseless to the human imagination. Remember,

For My thoughts are not your thoughts, neither are your ways My ways (Isaiah 55:8).

You need to be sure, though, that it is the voice of God you are hearing and obeying.

GOD NEEDED A PRIEST

You do need to get to a stage where you would willingly dedicate your unborn child to the service of God, if this is in His mind. This is the point to which Hannah got to before she conceived her long-awaited baby.

> **In bitterness of soul Hannah wept much and prayed to the LORD. And she made a vow, saying, "O LORD Almighty, if you will only look upon your servant's misery and remember me, and not forget your servant but give her a son, then I will give him to the LORD for all the days of his life, and no razor will ever be used on his head (1 Samuel 1:10-11).**

In total submission to God, Hannah made a vow to give her child she conceives back to the Lord. Unknown to her, God needed a priest for Israel. Eli, the priest at the time, did not bring up his children in the way of the Lord. So, his children did not qualify for the priestly office. Samuel, the child that Hannah had been waiting and weeping for, would be the perfect candidate to succeed Eli.

If Hannah was not barren for a while, she might not have thought of dedicating the child to God. Hannah's barrenness was not her fault, neither was it the fault of her husband or anybody else.

> But to Hannah He gave a double portion because He loved her, and the LORD had closed her womb (1 Samuel 1:5).

The Lord closed Hannah's womb because He needed a prophet through whom He could speak to His people, Israel. He did not relent until He got a vow and a prayer of dedication from Hannah. If you are waiting on the Lord, you need to discern who is delaying your children from coming—God or the devil?

KEEP YOUR VOWS

Has the Lord asked you to dedicate your child to Him? Are you struggling with the idea? In spite of your desire to see your child become a Doctor or Lawyer, does the thought of dedicating your unborn child to God keep coming to your mind? If this is what the Lord is requiring from you, why not be obedient? After Hannah gave birth to Samuel and gave him back to the Lord, she was blessed with many more children. Hannah honoured the Lord with her vow.

> For this child I prayed, and the Lord has granted my petition which I asked of Him. Therefore I also have lent him to the Lord; as long as he lives he shall be lent to the Lord (1 Samuel 1:27-28, NKJV).

Note that Hannah did not change her mind about giving Samuel to the Lord after her petition was granted. In the same way, you will need to keep your vow to Him when He answers you. Hannah kept her promise. As a result, each time she and her husband went to see Samuel, Eli the priest prophesied God's blessings on them and their descendants. She could have ended up with only Samuel if she had not dedicated him to God's service.

> **Each year his mother made him a little robe and took it to him when she went up with her husband to offer the annual sacrifice. Eli would bless Elkanah and his wife, saying, "May the LORD give you children by this woman to take the place of the one she prayed for and gave to the LORD." Then they would go home. And the LORD was gracious to Hannah; she conceived and gave birth to three sons and two daughters. Meanwhile, the boy Samuel grew up in the presence of the LORD (1 Samuel 2:19-21).**

I encourage you to carefully consider all the verses of 1 Samuel Chapters 1 and 2, especially if you have had a child before and want more (or you have been told that you have secondary infertility). Read these verses prayerfully, asking the Lord to reveal His heart to you. Open your heart to receive God's directive and be obedient to what He is leading you to do.

It is not an easy thing to give away your only child to the Lord — the child that you have desired for so many years. You would not even want anything to touch the child let alone leaving him with a priest in another town—a priest that could not control his own children! Hannah did. She did not allow the emotional bonding between her only child and herself to rob her of God's additional blessings. She did not care about missing out on her son's growth and developmental milestones. She honoured her vow. She left Samuel with Eli when he was young.

After he was weaned, she took the boy with her, young as he was, along with a three-year-old bull, an ephah of flour and a skin of wine, and brought him to the house of the LORD at Shiloh (1 Samuel 1:24).

Think again, is the Lord requiring something from you?

CHAPTER 4

Confronted By The Enemy

I joined my fiancé in England one and a half years after my conversion. Soon afterwards, we got married and started trying for a baby.

Two months later, I had a dream. In the dream, I went to the loo only to discover that my period had started. I was surprised to discover I was not yet pregnant. A lady had entered the toilet with me but I had not taken any notice of her. When she saw the surprise on my face, she said, "Why are you surprised to see your period again? Don't you know that you can never get pregnant?"

I was totally confused and baffled. I just stood there wandering in my heart who she was and whether she meant what she said. Menstruation is a private matter; moreover, how did she know the reason for my surprise? At that point, she introduced herself as the demonic spirit on assignment to ensure that I never have children. "Don't ever expect to carry any pregnancy or have children of your own," she said.

What a bold confrontation, I said to myself. As I stood pondering on the things the lady had said, she walked away and I woke up. I was shocked to discover that my period had actually started.

STRENGTHENED BY THE WORD

After the dream, I realised there was a battle at hand. Strangely, I was not scared but furious. I recalled the Lord's promise that He will never leave nor forsake me.

> **Never will I leave you; never will I forsake you. So we say with confidence, The Lord is my helper; I will not be afraid. What can man do to me? (Hebrews 13:5b-6).**

I was graciously strengthened by His word. *"What can man do to me?"* Even though demons are *different* from man, they are *lower* than man because they are fallen angels. The Bible teaches that man is higher than angels and lower than God.

> **What is man that you are mindful of him, the son of man that you care for him? You made him a little lower than the heavenly beings and crowned him with glory and honor (Psalm 8:4-5).**

If man who is on the same level with me cannot harm me, what can ordinary fallen angels (demons) do to me? Psalm 18:34 says,

He trains my hands for battle; my arms can bend a bow of bronze.

He teaches me to declare war against those who were incensed against me. When I woke up from the dream, I was furious at the boldness of this demon to confront me in the way it did. In response, I declared war against the evil spirit. I was determined not to give up until victory was secured in the spiritual and physical realms. Even though the demonic spirit, represented by the woman, introduced herself and her purpose, I refused to be moved.

Who is he who speaks and it comes to pass, when the Lord has not commanded it? (Lamentations 3:37, NKJV).

I knew the Lord had not ordained barrenness in my life neither has He ordained it in any other woman's life. For the bible says,

And none will miscarry or be barren in your land. I will give you a full life span (Exodus 23:26).

Experiencing a *delay* in having children is not God's *denial*. If the Lord has said it, He will surely bring it to pass. Micah, David's wife was the only childless woman in the entire Bible because she despised her husband for dancing in the presence of God and the people in an undignified way.

God desires our worship. If you look down on someone who is worshipping God, you might be threading on dangerous ground. The person need not be your husband but could be a relative or friend.

If you are in the habit of hindering your husband from worshipping and serving his Maker, you better watch out. We were created for God's pleasure. As we worship Him, we bring Him pleasure. Are you guilty of the 'sin of Micah?' Stop and ask for God's forgiveness because whoever despises the worship of Almighty God may not go unpunished. Such sins, in my, opinion can prevent a woman from conceiving and giving birth.

CHAPTER 5

Don't Crack The Wall

I had another dream months after the demonic confrontation in my sleep. In it, I was pregnant and I went to the antenatal clinic. There, I saw some strange-looking people walking on their heads. These beings put me on an hospital trolley and took me straight into the theatre for an abortion. When I woke up, I began to bleed.

I was troubled by the dream. How could this be happening to a Spirit-filled, tongue-speaking child of God? I took time to inquire from the Lord the cause of these occurrences. What I learnt from God and His word was quite revealing.

I discovered that these things could happen if the 'hedge' God puts around us is broken. With this insight, I began to search the scriptures and read books about deliverance. I concluded that this would be the way out of my predicament. However, I found out that there were sins in my life that I had not confessed.

The devil, who is the accuser of the brethren, is able to use hidden sins against you. He knows that God cannot stand anything filthy and would take the opportunity to build a case against you. If you are living perpetually in sin, you are casting away God's hedge of protection that is over you and the enemy will strike. Whenever the enemy wants to attack, he looks for loopholes to capitalise upon. If the wall is intact, then there is no way for him to get in.

COHABITATION

One of the issues in my life at the time that needed correction was that, prior to marriage, I was cohabiting with my fiancé. I was a young Christian when I came to join him in London and we thought the 'introduction' between the two families meant marriage. The Holy Spirit revealed to us that this was wrong. We spoke to our pastor about it and decided to put it right without delay. I know that as far as the east is from the west, so has the Lord forgiven and forgotten our sin.

Many times the children of Israel disobeyed God and He allowed them to be punished at the hands of their enemies. If you need help to put things right, ask the Holy Spirit to help you. He is your helper. You can also seek help and guidance from ministers of the gospel. Do it right now.

The Bible says,

Submit yourselves, then, to God. Resist the devil, and he will flee from you (James 4:7).

When you keep the commandments of God, you are submitted to him. Only then can you be successful in your battle against the enemy. The sons of Sceva tried to cast out demons and the evil spirits attacked them. They ran out of the house naked and wounded. If you try to resist the devil without obeying God's commandments, you are endangering yourself because Satan will have the legal ground to oppress you. Sin is of the devil and whoever sins is legally bound to be attacked by the devil.

Some Jews who went around driving out evil spirits tried to invoke the name of the Lord Jesus over those who were demon-possessed. They would say, "In the name of Jesus, whom Paul preaches, I command you to come out." Seven sons of Sceva, a Jewish chief priest, were doing this. One day the evil spirit answered them, "Jesus I know, and I know about Paul, but who are you?" Then the man who had the evil spirit jumped on them and overpowered them all. He gave them such a beating that they ran out of the house naked and bleeding (Act 19:13-16).

ABORTION

Another sin that is very common today is the deliberate termination of pregnancies.

> **Hear the word of the LORD, you rulers of Sodom; listen to the law of our God, you people of Gomorrah! "The multitude of your sacrifices -- what are they to me?" says the LORD. "I have more than enough of burnt offerings, of rams and the fat of fattened animals; I have no pleasure in the blood of bulls and lambs and goats. When you come to appear before me, who has asked this of you, this trampling of my courts? Stop bringing meaningless offerings! Your incense is detestable to me. New Moons, Sabbaths and convocations - I cannot bear your evil assemblies. Your New Moon festivals and your appointed feasts my soul hates. They have become a burden to me; I am weary of bearing them. When you spread out your hands in prayer, I will hide my eyes from you; even if you offer many prayers, I will not listen. Your hands are full of blood; wash and make yourselves clean. Take your evil deeds out of my sight! Stop doing wrong (Isaiah 1:10-16).**

According to this scripture, whenever someone aborts a pregnancy, the person's worship, sacrifices, praises and thanksgiving, which are supposed to rise up to God as a sweet smelling aroma, become abominable to Him. God ceases to derive pleasure from such worship; they become futile to Him.

Don't Crack the Wall

God cannot endure iniquity because He is holy and His throne is adorned with holiness. It becomes impossible for Him to build His holy throne in the midst of such praises and worship. Our God cannot behold or endure iniquity so He refuses to show His face. This implies that blessings are not released.

Our God is very compassionate and merciful. He does not enjoy seeing us suffering. At the same time, He cannot behold iniquity. So, He turns His face away when we sin, especially when they are not confessed and are left to linger for a long time.

Surely the arm of the LORD is not too short to save, nor his ear too dull to hear. But your iniquities have separated you from your God; your sins have hidden his face from you, so that he will not hear. For your hands are stained with blood, your fingers with guilt. Your lips have spoken lies, and your tongue mutters wicked things (Isaiah 59:1-3).

If I had cherished sin in my heart, the Lord would not have listened (Psalm 66:18).

The Lord said emphatically in Isaiah 1:15 that,

When you spread out your hands in prayer, I will hide my eyes from you; even if you offer many prayers, I will not listen. Your hands are full of blood.

Even if many prayers are made, God will refuse to answer if the hands are full of blood — the blood of aborted children. Both the carrier of the pregnancy and those who help to perform the abortion are guilty before God. You could be a doctor, nurse or midwife that helped someone to get rid of *an* unwanted pregnancy or you may have paid for someone to undergo an abortion or you may have advised someone to abort a baby, you are guilty of shedding blood and of taking undue advantage of the innocent and helpless.

No child deserves to have his or her life terminated prematurely. Some claim that as long as the foetus is aborted within six weeks, it is okay because the embryo does not have a heart at that stage. This, however, is not accurate, because the egg and sperm, after fusion, divides into balls of cells within 48 hours. The different parts of these cells would later develop into the babies different organs. It has also been recorded that the heart starts to beat from three weeks of pregnancy **(Practical Parenting October 1997 edition).**

Some say that the embryo cannot feel the pain of abortion at the early stage of pregnancy. However, it has been recorded that the nervous system starts developing from three weeks. Even if these beliefs are true, it does not make it right for anyone to take the life that God has given. To whom has the Lord given the authority to determine who lives and who does not?

CONTRACEPTION

What about the intra-uterine contraceptive device (IUCD)? Many people use this form of contraception without considering the ethical issues surrounding the way it works. Fertilisation takes place in the fallopian tubes. The fertilised egg travels down to the uterus to be embedded there. The role of the coil (otherwise known as IUCD) is to prevent the fertilised egg from embedding. This boils down to bloodshed. Thanks be to Jesus Christ who has not come to judge and condemn us. There is a new IUCD that prevents pregnancy through the hormone progesterone it carries. This according to medical research does not cause abortion.

Come now, let us reason together, says the LORD. Though your sins are like scarlet, they shall be as white as snow; though they are red as crimson, they shall be like wool. If you are willing and obedient, you will eat the best from the land (Isaiah 1:18,19).

Again, the gift of God is not like the result of the one man's sin: The judgment followed one sin and brought condemnation, but the gift followed many trespasses and brought justification (Romans 5:16).

Ephesians 2:4-10 lays more emphasis on the grace and mercy of God;

But because of his great love for us, God, who is rich in mercy, made us alive with Christ even when we were dead in transgressions--it is by grace you have been saved. And God raised us up with Christ and seated us with him in the heavenly realms in Christ Jesus, in order that in the coming ages he might show the incomparable riches of his grace, expressed in his kindness to us in Christ Jesus. For it is by grace you have been saved, through faith--and this not from yourselves, it is the gift of God-- not by works, so that no one can boast. For we are God's workmanship, created in Christ Jesus to do good works, which God prepared in advance for us to do.

PETTY SINS

You might not have engaged in cohabitation or abortion. Yours might be a 'petty' sin as some like to term it. All sins are the same before God, there is no small or big sin. Ask the Holy Spirit to search your heart and reveal any hindrance in it. The Lord does not want you to continue living in sin. He is calling out to you today.

We know that anyone born of God does not continue to sin; the one who was born of God keeps him safe, and the evil one cannot harm him. (1 John 5:18)

There is nowhere one can hide for God. He even knows whatever we attempt to hide from Him. The Psalmist said,

> **Where can I go from your Spirit? Where can I flee from your presence? If I go up to the heavens, you are there; if I make my bed in the depths, you are there. If I rise on the wings of the dawn, if I settle on the far side of the sea, even there your hand will guide me, your right hand will hold me fast. If I say, "Surely the darkness will hide me and the light become night around me," even the darkness will not be dark to you; the night will shine like the day, for darkness is as light to you (Psalm 139:7-12).**

He knows all that you have done wrong, yet He is merciful and gracious enough to reconcile you to Himself. He said, "even if your sins are as red as crimson they shall be as white as snow." No matter how bad the sin might look, He is willing to forgive and cleanse you.

Deliberate termination of pregnancy can open the door to unclean spirits, especially the spirit of death, which manifests in form of barrenness and sometimes financial insufficiency. Once you have repented of the sin, you also need to pray against and take authority over the spirit of death, cast it out of your life, and renounce barrenness and poverty.

If you are not sure of what to do, you can follow these step. First *acknowledge and confess* your sin to God. Then ask God to *cleanse and purify* you according to His Word (1 John 1:9); ask Him to *remove all curses* of disobedience to His words. When you have done all of the above, *take authority* over the spirit of death and ask God to fill your life afresh with His Holy Spirit.

CHAPTER 6

Whose Report Will You Believe?

A few months after we started trying for a baby, I started to fret over the evil confession and prophecies the white garment prophets had pronounced over me. They had told me several times that I will never be able to have a child. One of them was so sure to the point of saying that even if I got pregnant, I would miscarry repeatedly. Another one said convincingly to my Dad (in my presence) "she cannot have any children. It will take a miracle from God for her to have a child. In any case, *it is impossible* that she bears any."

MY HUMAN APPROACH

When I remembered all these negative words, I knew there was battle ahead but I did not have any clue how tough the battle would be. I became so worried and attempted to solve the problem physically. Little did I know that a spiritual problem does not have physical solutions. The Bible declares in II Corinthians 10:3-4,

> **For though we live in the world, we do not wage war as the world does. The weapons we fight with are not the weapons of the world. On the contrary, they have divine power to demolish strongholds.**

I knew there were some fertility problems that medical science can solve. But in my own case, I realised that it required a divine solution. Notwithstanding, I went to see our family doctor who said that before I could be referred to the hospital for investigation, I must have tried to conceive for at least one full year. I went home hoping it would happen before the end of the year. I could not wait another month, let alone a whole year.

AFTER A YEAR

At the end of year one, nothing happened. I began to feel sorry for myself. I felt helpless not knowing how many more waiting years were ahead of me. Our family doctor now referred me to the hospital. My husband and I went through a series of investigations. He was found to be okay, but I was told that my hormones and other reproduction features were fine but both of my fallopian tubes were closed. I had a surgical investigation to visualise my womb (laparascopy and dye). My legs became wobbly as I walked into the consulting room for the result. As the consultant revealed her findings, I knew I was in for big trouble. The result read, "fallopian tubes bilaterally closed."

That meant my eggs and my husband's sperm could never meet in the right place. The fertilised egg could continue to grow in the fallopian tube and result in a very critical condition because the tube will eventually rupture causing internal bleeding. If the condition is not attended to on time, it could lead to death. If it is promptly attended to, the fallopian tube will have to be removed, which will make conception impossible from the human point of view.

When I took the report to our family Doctor, she was unusually silent and then asked how old I was. After telling her, she was again silent for a while. Her silence confirmed that my condition required God's intervention and not man's. At this point, my faith began to rise.

I thought of the God of Abraham, Isaac and Jacob and became peaceful. I was convinced that if I took my request to Him in prayer He would do something about it. I believed that He would either open the tubes or give me brand new ones. I did not even want to figure out how He would do it. All I knew was that I was going to give birth to a child.

This is what the LORD says - he who made a way through the sea, a path through the mighty waters, who drew out the chariots and horses, the army

and reinforcements together, and they lay there, never to rise again, extinguished, snuffed out like a wick: "Forget the former things; do not dwell on the past. See, I am doing a new thing! Now it springs up; do you not perceive it? I am making a way in the desert and streams in the wasteland (Isaiah 43:16-19).

He is the Lord who makes a way in the wilderness and through the sea. He said that we should not consider the things of old because He will do a new thing. I did not even consider the old blocked fallopian tubes because I knew that He specialises in doing new things. I knew that when He visits me, He would create new fallopian tubes in my womb.

My prayer for you as you read this book is that the Lord God, who is mighty in power, will do a new thing in your life. No matter how great the trouble you may be facing right now, the Lord is able to take care of it. The Psalmist said that He is mightier than the mighty waves of the sea and the wind.

ANOTHER THREE MONTHS

Blocked tubes is one of the leading causes of infertility in women but with new developments in technology, some of them are operable. The doctors were not sure how badly damaged my tubes were so it was difficult to say whether they were operable or not. In view of this, I was scheduled for another investigation three months later. I was told that this investigation is more reliable than the first.

The investigation is called *hystero-salpingography*, involving the introduction of dye into the uterus and visualisation with x-ray as the dye travels from the uterus through the length of the fallopian tubes. If there was any obstruction, then the dye would not travel the whole length of the tubes.

On the day of the investigation, my hopes were high. I had confessed that God would overturn the doctors report—and that was exactly what He did. They watched the dye travel the length of the tubes without any obstruction on both ends. To be sure, they repeated the test again and again only to come to the same conclusion—that my tubes were in perfect condition.

At last, God had done something about my tubes! I had experienced a miracle! I do not know what He did, but prior to the visit to the clinic, I had a dream in which someone carried out a successful surgical operation on me. I was confident that my fallopian tubes were potent and in good condition, and the result of the doctor's investigation confirmed this. I went home full of faith, expecting to conceive without any further delay. But it did not happen as I had expected.

I do not know what your own ups and downs have been on the journey of childbirth; what medical names doctors have given to your condition. Or are they yet to find a name for it? Have you been told that there is nothing anyone can do to help you? The word of the Lord to you today is this,

> **Come to me, all you who are weary and burdened, and I will give you rest. Take my yoke upon you and learn from me, for I am gentle and humble in heart, and you will find rest for your souls. For my yoke is easy and my burden is light (Matthew 11:28-30).**

The angel of the Lord said to Mary,

> **For nothing is impossible with God (Luke 1:37).**

Let Mary's reply be your proclamation from today onwards.

> **I am the Lord's servant, Mary answered. May it be to me as you have said. Then the angel left her (Luke 1:38).**

The word of the Lord to you is that none shall be barren in the land. Your reply to this word should be, *"let it be unto me according to your word."* He is a God of possibilities and no condition is greater than Him; no condition is too much for Him to handle. Besides, Jesus took them all to the cross (Isaiah 53 says, *"He carried your grief, sorrows and pains to the cross."*) Medical conditions such as *endometriosis, hormonal imbalance, blocked fallopian tubes, fibroids, secondary infertility* (due to unknown causes), *primary infertility*, husband's *low sperm count, anovulation* (absence of ovulation) etc, all these Jesus carried to the cross for you. He was smitten, afflicted and beaten for your diseases. You need not carry them anymore by yourself. He carried them all on the cross once and for all. His victory is now *your* victory.

God does not delight in afflicting people with diseases for He says in Exodus 15:22-26,

> **Then Moses led Israel from the Red Sea and they went into the Desert of Shur. For three days they traveled in the desert without finding water. When they came to Marah, they could not drink its water because it was bitter. (That is why the place is called Marah.) So the people grumbled against Moses, saying "What are we to drink?" Then Moses cried out to the LORD, and the LORD showed him a piece of wood. He threw it into the water, and the water became sweet. There the LORD made a decree and a law for them, and there he tested he said, "If you listen carefully to the voice of the LORD your God and do what is right in his eyes, if you pay attention to his commands and keep all his decrees, I will not bring on you any of the diseases I brought on the Egyptians, for I am the LORD, who heals you."**

WHAT ARE YOU SEEING AND SAYING?

If the doctors are seeing infirmities, infertility and barrenness, what are you seeing? Are you seeing what they are seeing as well? Are you confessing their own words about your situation? Or are you seeing what God is seeing about that situation? Are your confessions and affirmations what He has said in His word?

Whose report will you believe? Is it the doctor's report that has labelled you infertile, the world's report that refers to you as barren or the Lord's report that has called you a joyful mother of children? Prophet Isaiah realised the authenticity of the word of God and said that he would believe the report of the Lord. The report of the Lord to you is that you will not be afflicted with any disease of the Egyptians and "by the stripes" of Jesus Christ you are healed. I challenge you to begin to confess the word of God in line with your situation. When people speak negatively to you about the situation, reject it and confess positively. Do not be overwhelmed and carried away by the magnitude of your condition but be fully persuaded in God and in what He can do.

CHAPTER 7

Be Quiet

Day after day, month after month and year after year, I expected to become pregnant but nothing happened. I hoped that one day I would wake up to my miracle. The waiting period seemed longer than it really was. I fasted and prayed fervently for a breakthrough. Expectantly, I attended church and miracle services but there were no changes. Other people around me often had testimonies to share but I did not have any. "Oh that the Lord will do a new thing in my life as well" was my usual plea. There were times that, out of frustration, I got impatient with God. At a time I stopped communicating with Him.

I must admit that this stage of despair could be very dangerous. If care is not taken, one can begin to murmur against God. Satan will try to capitalise on the negative feelings. He will bring evil thoughts about your Maker to your heart. These thoughts, even if not uttered, are very destructive. The smallest thought in the deepest place of your heart is loud enough for God to hear. He is the all-knowing God.

I would not deny that I grumbled against the Lord during my early waiting period. But once the Holy Spirit made me realise what I was doing wrong, I confessed my sin and asked God for forgiveness.

ISRAEL'S REACTIONS IN THE WILDERNESS

As I began the discipline of reading through the bible in one year. I read about the Israelites' deliverance from Egypt with God's powerful arm. Following their deliverance, they began to murmur against God; they made countless complaints against the Lord who brought them out of the land of slavery.

But who are you, O man, to talk back to God? "Shall what is formed say to him who formed it, `Why did you make me like this?' " Does not the potter have the right to make out of the same lump of clay some pottery for noble purposes and some for common use? (Romans 9:20-21).

Instead of asking God many questions that will lead to complaints, plead for His mercy. The Bible says in Roman 9:15

For he says to Moses, "I will have mercy on whom I have mercy, and I will have compassion on whom I have compassion."

Also in Numbers 14:1-4,

That night all the people of the community raised their voices and wept aloud. All the Israelites grumbled against Moses and Aaron, and the whole assembly said to them, "If only we had died in Egypt! Or in this desert! Why is the LORD bringing us to this land only to let us fall by the sword? Our wives and children will be taken as plunder. Wouldn't it be better for us to go back to Egypt?" And they said to each other, "We should choose a leader and go back to Egypt."

After the Israelites received the report of the land that the Lord had promised them, they complained, murmured and grumbled against Moses their leader and God. They did not for a minute consider the great and mighty things that the Lord had done for them. The only thing they could see at that moment was the battle before them. They were short-sighted and could not see beyond the difficulties they had to pass through. They could not see the victory and blessings of the promised land that lied beyond the war. They preferred death in Egypt as slaves to dying by the sword in Canaan. Every problem they encountered in the wilderness was an occasion to murmur against God.

In the desert the whole community grumbled against Moses and Aaron. The Israelites said to them, "If only we had died by the LORD's hand in Egypt! There we sat around pots of meat and ate all

the food we wanted, but you have brought us out into this desert to starve this entire assembly to death." Then the LORD said to Moses, "I will rain down bread from heaven for you. The people are to go out each day and gather enough for that day. In this way I will test them and see whether they will follow my instructions (Exodus 16:2-4).

The Israelites complained against Moses; they wanted bread and meat as they had in Egypt. Moses went to God on their behalf and the Lord answered them and gave them manna and quail. They eventually got tired of the manna and began to grumble again.

The rabble with them began to crave other food, and again the Israelites started wailing and said, "If only we had meat to eat! We remember the fish we ate in Egypt at no cost--also the cucumbers, melons, leeks, onions and garlic. But now we have lost our appetite; we never see anything but this manna!" The manna was like coriander seed and looked like resin. The people went around gathering it, and then ground it in a handmill or crushed it in a mortar. They cooked it in a pot or made it into cakes. And it tasted like something made with olive oil. When the dew settled on the camp at night, the manna also came down. Moses heard the people of every family wailing, each at the entrance to his tent. The LORD became exceedingly angry, and Moses was troubled. He asked the LORD, "Why have you brought this trouble on your servant? What have I done to displease you that you put the burden of all these people on me? Did I conceive all these people? Did I give them birth? Why do you tell me to carry them in my arms, as a nurse carries an infant, to the land you promised on oath to their forefathers? Where can I get meat for all these people? They keep wailing to me, `Give us meat to eat!' I cannot carry all these people by myself; the burden is too heavy for me. If this is how you are going to treat me, put me to death right now--if I have found favor in your eyes--and do not let me face my own ruin (Num. 11:4-15).

Because of the Israelites' rebellion and the hardness of heart, the Lord was angry at that generation. The Lord swore in His wrath that they would not enter the Promised Land. A forty days' journey took them forty years. Trusting God for children may be your own wilderness. What you do in your wilderness will determine how easy and early you will come out of it.

So, as the Holy Spirit says: "Today, if you hear his voice, do not harden your hearts as you did in the rebellion, during the time of testing in the desert, where your fathers tested and tried me and for forty years saw what I did. That is why I was angry with that generation, and I said, `Their hearts are always going astray, and they have not known my ways.' So I declared on oath in my anger, `They shall never enter my rest' (Hebrews 3:7-11).

Are you also like the Israelites? Have you grumbled and murmured against God endlessly because of your slight affliction? Must you always grumble to make your request known to God? Make your request known in the right way. Philippians 4:6-7 says,

Do not be anxious about anything, but in everything, by prayer and petition (supplication — NKJV), with thanksgiving, present your requests to God. And the peace of God, which transcends all understanding, will guard your hearts and your minds in Christ Jesus.

When you are anxious, the pressure could get you to the point of uttering wrong words to God. The bible says, "in everything", and that includes when things are not going the way you want them to go, even when nothing has happened after praying and fasting. In everything by prayer and petition or supplication with thanksgiving let your request be made known to God, not with grumbling, murmuring or complaining.

The word supplication comes from the Latin word *'supplicaire,'* meaning to kneel down. The family dictionary defines it as asking humbly and submissively. The scripture went further to say that our requests should be made with thanksgiving. This means that before your request is granted begin to thank the Lord for it. Thanksgiving is an act of rendering gratitude for a divine goodness (*The Family Dictionary*).

> **The Lord is good to those who wait for Him, to the soul who seeks Him. It is good that one should hope and wait quietly (Lamentation 3:25-26, NKJV).**

Let your spirit not grumble against your Maker while you wait on Him for your child. Wait quietly on Him and let your spirit be calm within you. When you have made your request known to Him with a humble, submissive and quiet spirit, give to Him gratitude for what you are hoping He will do for you.

> **And the peace of God that passes all understanding shall protect your heart and mind (Philippians 4:7, NKJV).**

> **I waited patiently for the lord and He inclined to me and heard my cry. (Psalm 40:1, NKJV).**

If you wait patiently, He will listen to your cry. I used to be anxious near the time of my menstrual cycle. Most of the time I refused to get out of bed thinking my slightest movement will prompt its arrival. It did not have to be like this. Be anxious for nothing. Do not even give any thought to your period coming or not.

Blessed are all those who wait for Him. (Isaiah 30:18b, NKJV).

WAIT PATIENTLY

There is a blessing that comes with waiting on the Lord. It involves putting your trust in God. If you do not trust that He can meet your need, you cannot wait for Him. When you visit a restaurant and the waitress comes to take your order, you don't go into the kitchen to prepare the food yourself. You wait at your table for the waitress. The only reason why you waited for the waitress was because you trusted that she would bring your ordered meal. Waiting for the Lord involves putting your complete trust in Him. The bible says in Psalm 2:12b,

Blessed are all those who put their trust in Him. (NKJV).

However, it is not enough to only wait for Him, you need to wait patiently as well. At times, what you are waiting for might not come as quickly as you expect. This is the reason why you need patience.

Three other blessings come with waiting for the Lord patiently. Firstly, you shall inherit the earth, that is, have all that you have ever wanted. Secondly, your enemies shall be wiped out before you and thirdly, you shall enjoy abundant peace.

Rest in the Lord and wait patiently for Him; do not

fret because of him who prospers in his way, because of the man who brings wicked schemes to pass, for evil doers shall be cut off but those who wait on the Lord they shall inherit the earth but the meek shall inherit the earth, and shall delight themselves in the abundant of peace (Psalm 37:7,9,11, NKJV).

TESTIMONY OF KING DAVID

Finally, let us learn a few lessons from the testimony of King David who waited patiently for the Lord as described in Psalm 40:1-3,

I waited patiently for the LORD; He turned to me and heard my cry. He lifted me out of the slimy pit, out of the mud and mire; he set my feet on a rock and gave me a firm place to stand. He put a new song in my mouth, a hymn of praise to our God. Many will see and fear and put their trust in the LORD.

The Lord inclined His ears to him and heard his cry. (The Lord paid particular attention to David's cry). The Lord brought him out of his problem. The Lord strengthened him to stand. The Lord established him. He put a new song in David's mouth. Many that will hear the testimony will also put their trust in God.

MY PRAYER FOR YOU

You will not forfeit your miracle because of grumbling. You will not extend your waiting period through your murmuring. The Lord will help you to

step into supernatural patience as you wait for Him. As you wait patiently for Him He will incline His ears to your cry and listen to your prayer. As He hears the voice of your cry, I pray that the Lord will reach out from His Holy place to rescue you from the pangs of the enemy and problem of childlessness that presents itself as if there is no help for you. The Lord Himself will reach out to you to pull you out of that miry clay, He will also set your feet upon the rock of Jesus Christ and establish you. I also pray that your song will also change from that of supplication to a song of thanksgiving. From your testimony many shall come to know the Lord. Amen.

As much as praying and fasting are important, so also is waiting for God quietly and patiently.

CHAPTER 8

The Humiliation

It was frustrating to discover that I could not have children even though I desired them. I felt as if I was an abnormal person, especially when medical tests revealed that I was the one with the problem.

This frustration resulted in low self-esteem and self-worth. I felt intimidated and offended by almost everything people said or did to me even when they meant no harm. I even felt intimidated by children! I began to see myself as a good-for-nothing woman who had failed in her role to be a perfect wife. I found it difficult interacting with people because I did not think I would mean anything to anyone. I also did not want them to notice my desperation for children.

You need not feel this way because nobody can create life. You are not capable of bringing about conception. The fact that you are waiting on God for children does not make you inferior to any one else, not even those with children. This is the point that the Lord brought me to by His power. You are who you are in the Lord Jesus Christ. No matter what the problem is, the Bible says in Psalm 139:14 that you are fearfully and wonderfully made.

What you are going through at the moment does not have anything to do with your ministerial status or position. My husband was a minister during that time and still is.

It is true that people will sometimes deliberately say and do things to provoke you, especially if you are from Africa. In-laws will consider it bad luck for their family. They will try to frustrate the woman so that she can leave and allow their son to remarry. If the wife decides to endure the frustrations and humiliation, the husband is encouraged to marry another woman who could bear children.

Are you facing this kind of problem? This is the word of the Lord to you.

He grants the barren woman a home, like a joyful mother of children (Psalm 113:9, NKJV).

The Lord will grant you a home that no one can disrupt. No one will be able to displace you from where the Lord has set you. No one will be able to unseat you from your God-given home. If the Lord has indeed joined you to your husband no man can put you apart. The Bible says

A three fold cord is not easily broken (Ecclesiastes 4:12).

Hannah endured severe provocation from Penninah, but she decided not to enter into argument or keep malice with her. She did not even report Penninah to Elkanah, their husband, even though she knew he would always listen to her. She by-passed the entire human avenue that could be her weapons to fight Penninah. Instead, she went directly to God, the highest authority.

Something that interested me about Penninah was her negative "motivational gift" that forced Hannah out of her comfort zone, unto her knees and into her blessing. In this light, I am glad that Penninah provoked Hannah. Penninah literally drove her into the presence of God. Hannah poured out her grievances before Him and as a result, something miraculous happened in her life. The Lord remembered her and she conceived. Had Penninah known that her provocation would result in Hannah's child bearing, she would not have done it at all.

Had Satan known that crucifying Jesus would bring redemption and victory to the entire human race, and glory to Jesus, he would not have crucified the Lamb of God.

> We do, however, speak a message of wisdom among the mature, but not the wisdom of this age or of the rulers of this age, who are coming to nothing. No, we speak of God's secret wisdom, a wisdom that has been hidden and that God

destined for our glory before time began. *None of the rulers of this age understood it, for if they had, they would not have crucified the Lord of glory.* However, as it is written: "No eye has seen, no ear has heard, no mind has conceived what God has prepared for those who love him" (I Corinthians 2:6-9).

God works in mysterious ways. Who are the people that you run to when things are rough? When your in-laws are provoking you, do you run to your husband, your friends or your parents for comfort? When your husband provokes you, do you run to your in-laws and family for solace?

The Bible says that the arm of flesh will fail you. You cannot run to God and be ashamed. Let the "Penninahs" in your life drive you to God. Do not allow unforgiveness, hatred, bitterness, malice or anxiety to keep you from your miracle.

Your own Penninah may not be a person but could be a provocative curse or aggravation to your childlessness. Go before the Lord and pour out your spirit and the Lord will surely remember you as He remembered Hannah.

As the Lord also took away the reproach of Elizabeth, so will the He take away yours.

After this his wife Elizabeth became pregnant and for five months remained in seclusion. "The Lord has done this for me," she said. "In these days he has shown his favor and taken away my disgrace among the people (Luke 1:24, 25).

BE ENVIOUS OF NO ONE

As you wait on the Lord, life can generate many questions, especially when you meet other pregnant women. In my case, I asked, "What are they doing right?"; "What am I doing wrong?"; "Why would others conceive and not me?" I began to get envious of whoever was pregnant around me. Anytime I heard that someone was pregnant I used to think, *Oh another person is pregnant again, what about me? When would I carry mine?*

All these thoughts are rooted in envy; they are not from God. Love does not envy. Envy is not of God.

Love is patient, love is kind. *It does not envy*, **it does not boast, it is not proud (1 Corinthians 13:4)**

Let us not become conceited, provoking and *envying* **each other (Galatians 5:26)**

Envy is like a disease that destroys the heart because it brings all sorts of evil thoughts to one's mind. The Lord made me realise that this is an unacceptable behaviour in His kingdom.

Following this, I went before the Lord to make my heart known to Him. The fact was that I did not enjoy envying. I repented before God and He forgave me. I also asked Him for special grace to overcome this problem. From that time on, when I heard that someone was pregnant, I would rejoice with them knowing that one-day they will rejoice with me.

If you are facing the same problem I faced, I believe you can overcome it through the power of the Almighty God. Ask Him to forgive you and help you to overcome envy. Ask God to condition your heart to good thoughts and love.

CHAPTER 9

I Thought God Was In It

After the various medical investigations we endured, my husband and I were told that there was nothing wrong with our reproductive organs. Everything was perfect and normal. In light of this, we were told that we did not require any treatment. Consequently, we were discharged from the gynae clinic and were advised, however, to go for In-Vitro Fertilisation (IVF). This, according to them, was our last resort.

The waiting list for the IVF was eighteen months. When I heard this, I thought, *I would give birth before then*. I was so sure that I would not need the treatment. Time went by—days, weeks and months—but I was still hopeful. I was sure in my heart that God would not let me down.

We ended up waiting for 2½ years for the treatment. Even then, I still believed that late in the midnight hour God would turn around and work in my favour. Eventually we received a letter that it was our turn for the treatment. We were called to a meeting with the specialists and over a hundred other couples who would be going through the treatment as well.

When I first received the letter, I was a bit disappointed because I expected God to have intervened without having to go through the treatment. It was a real test of my faith that I still was not pregnant at the time. I did not like the thought of having my children formed by a scientist in a test-tube but I wanted children so desperately.

I spoke to a family friend who advised me to go for the treatment but never to tell anyone about it. I was so desperate for a child that I did not mind God using the IVF treatment to produce one. I believe this was a passive way to make such a great decision. Also, because of our desperation, we hoped that God would change His principle. (God will not share His glory with any man). We did not consider the ethical or moral issues surrounding the treatment until we started encountering them. However, we did not compromise our faith.

CONTEMPLATING IVF?

My heart goes out to every couple who went into marriage with the intention of procreating early in the relationship only to discover that they could not due to problems with their reproductive organs. Having to wait endlessly can be very frustrating.

With new developments in the treatment of infertility, it is so easy to undergo treatment without considering the ethical, moral or legal issues surrounding it. This new treatment takes away the sacredness and privacy of fusion in the mother's womb. The sperm is collected through masturbation, which, in our judgement, is not an acceptable practise. My husband refused this method of sperm collection. Instead he was offered a spermicidal-free condom.

Another issue which requires consideration is the involvement of a third party in the marriage for the process of procreation. This could either be by obtaining a donor sperm, egg or surrogate mother.

I am not against technology. I do believe it is a sign of God's grace and it is part of taking dominion as God commanded us, but when considering a treatment such as this you need to ask yourself certain questions: *How would it affect the unborn child? How would it affect my society? How would it affect my relationship with God?*

I do not wish to discuss this issue in detail as it is beyond the scope of this book. But, in whatever situation you find yourself, be sure that only God takes *all* the glory; not some, not most, but *all* the glory.

We did not consider the cost aspect of this complicated treatment until we were about to start. We were told the treatment would cost £2000, plus we need to purchase medications worth £800, adding up to £2800. We could not afford the payment at the time. So, we started believing God for the money. Shortly after we started praying, we were informed that the treatment was free for those living in our part of London. Our family doctor also agreed to prescribe the medication that I needed. I only had to pay a prescription fee of £25 for medication worth £800. All these made us to believe that God had His hand in the treatment.

GOD'S HIDDEN WISDOM

I began to take the prescribed hormonal medication, which initially suppressed the ovary's normal cycle of egg production. Then I commenced another hormonal medication that stimulated the ovaries to produce more eggs than usual. After a little while, I was called in for a scan to enable the experts see if my ovaries had produced enough eggs. At least six eggs must be produced and retrieved to continue with the treatment. During the scan, it was discovered that my left ovary had produced four eggs while the right ovary had only produced one. It was explained that the only egg produced by my right ovary was useless because they would not be able to retrieve it due to the position of my right ovary to my right fallopian tube. Amazing!

It was concluded that I would have to stop the treatment and start all over again. I was told to wait for another two to three months before I could recommence the treatment.

I thank the Lord for the bible says in 1 Corinthians 2:5-10,

So that your faith may not rest on men's wisdom but on God's power. We do, however, speak a message of wisdom among the mature, but not the wisdom of this age or of the rulers of this age, who are coming to nothing. No, we speak of God's secret wisdom, a wisdom that has been hidden and that God destined for our glory before time began. None of the rulers of this age understood it, for if they had, they would not have crucified the Lord of glory. However, as it is written: *"No eye has seen, no ear has heard, no mind has conceived what God has prepared for those who love him"* **but God has revealed it to us by his Spirit. The Spirit searches all things, even the deep things of God.**

Thank God for His hidden wisdom in every situation of our lives. Even the Bible says that had Satan known, he would not have crucified the Lord of glory. Had Satan known the hidden wisdom of God, he would not have intercepted the IVF treatment. By the time God revealed His plan it was too late for the devil to change his mind. The devil is already sorry for what he has done to you.

The Bible says that,

A man's steps are directed by the Lord. How then can anyone understand his own way? (Proverbs 20:24).

Near the time of the treatment, my husband started to pray for five eggs to be produced from my ovaries. He did not realise that the treatment would be cancelled if the eggs were not more than five. He thought that if we had more than five eggs and all of them were fertilised, we would end up with more children than we wanted. He did not want any of the fertilised eggs to be deliberately destroyed because this would mean the destruction of life.

I was not aware that he had been praying for only five eggs otherwise I would have suggested that we prayed for at least six. This would have met the medical criteria for continuing the treatment. When the treatment stopped, I was disappointed and felt let down by God. I cried like a baby. I thought God was in the whole treatment but obviously, He was not. I had got it all wrong. God will not share His glory with any man.

> **I am the LORD; that is my name! I will not give my glory to another or my praise to idols. (Isaiah 42:8).**

I expected God to show up before the treatment but He did not. Thereafter, I thought He was going to use the IVF treatment, but it was painful to know that He did not show up during the treatment either. Just like He did to Lazarus, Jesus did not show up until he had been dead for four days despite the fact that He knew when Lazarus became ill.

Not only is He the Lord of the past but also Lord of the present and the future. That is why all glory belongs to Him. Nothing and no one can exalt itself above this Lord.

THE GREATEST CUDDLE

As I got the message that the treatment would cease and I would have to rest for a while, tears filled my eyes. I tried in vain to fight it back. I felt weak from discouragement. I thought His hand was in the whole process from the beginning. Apparently, not even His finger was in it. It was as if there would never be a way out for me.

As tears rolled down my eyes uncontrollably, I stood beside the telephone not knowing what to do or say or who to call for comfort. There was no friend around to comfort me and my husband was at work. There was no shoulder to lean and cry on. I was alone.

I then went into the bedroom, tucked myself into bed and began to cry convulsively. I kept asking, *"Why Lord?"* It was so painful. Even though I was under the duvet, I felt cold; I was almost shivering.

Then, all of a sudden, in-between sobs, I heard footsteps. My husband could not have returned from work so early, I thought. No one else lives in the flat with us. The steps kept coming closer and closer. I was not afraid. I just could not be bothered.

Eventually I felt the presence of someone on my bed and felt a warm cuddle wrap all around me. It was like the person had given me his shoulder to lean and weep on. That perfect opportunity finally arrived and I seized it. I leaned on Him and wept like a baby, irresistibly. *"But whose shoulder am I leaning on; whose arms are cuddling me?"*

In a matter of seconds, I began to feel an inner peace and I experienced a great calmness in my spirit. *"Have I been crying on the Lord's shoulder?"* Intuitively, I knew the Spirit of the Lord had walked into my bedroom to cuddle me. Without a word He brought me comfort for He is my Comforter. In the midst of the silence, He counselled me for He is my Counsellor; as my Helper He helped me through the most difficult moment of my life.

When no one was there to comfort me, He was there. No one could have done it better. No one could have fulfilled this role — not even my husband. Jesus indeed is my friend.

The Lord gave me a song there and then:

> The Lord was with me
> In the midst of my troubles
> The Lord was with me
> In the midst of it all
> He went through the pain
> He went through the sorrow
> He went through the heartache with me

I was never alone
In the midst of my troubles
The Lord was with me
The Lord strengthened me
In the midst of it all
Hallelujah (2ce)
The Lord was with me
In the midst of it all
The Lord cuddled me
The Lord upheld me
The Lord carried me
In the midst of it all © Toyin 2002

MY RESPONSE

In response, I said to Him, *"You'll always be my God even if I do not have a child. All my desperation for a child I leave in your capable arms."* Here is my favourite passage in the Bible that strengthened me and gave me power to move on:

Though the fig tree does not bud and there are no grapes on the vines, though the olive crop fails and the fields produce no food, though there are no sheep in the pen and no cattle in the stalls, yet I will rejoice in the LORD, I will be joyful in God my Savior. The Sovereign LORD is my strength; he makes my feet like the feet of a deer, he enables me to go on the heights (Habakkuk 3:17-19).

I had trusted God so much that I would not need the IVF treatment to bear children. Initially, when this seemed to fail, it was like a shattered trust. It did not dawn on me until I began to write this book that God had not at any time purposed to use IVF as a means to my having children.

Very early in my attempts to conceive a baby, the Lord had revealed to me that I was in bondage and that He will set me free through the Ministry that I was attending at the time. God had already told me where my help was but I did not recognise it. In other words, He had already given me the journey planner that would lead to my breakthrough (see page 12). My prayer for you is that God will help you to discern how and where He intends to bless you. This understanding will save you unnecessary heartache. It is of utmost importance that you know what God is saying in your situation.

You might have been through several fertility treatments without any fruitful outcome. The doctors might have said to you this is your last chance or there is nothing more they can do, but know that this is the time for God to step in.

And we know that in all things God works for the good of those who love Him, who have been called according to His purpose (Romans 8:28).

The fact that you have been told there is no more hope is not the end of the world. God will use the hopelessness to work miracles in your life as He has purposed. His thoughts towards you are of good thoughts and not of evil, thoughts to give you a hope and a future.

> **So that your faith might not rest on men's wisdom, but on God's power. We do, however, speak a message of wisdom among the mature, but not the wisdom of this age or of the rulers of this age, who are coming to nothing. No, we speak of God's secret wisdom, a wisdom that has been hidden and that God destined for our glory before time began. None of the rulers of this age understood it, for if they had, they would not have crucified the Lord of glory (I Corinthians 2:5-8).**

The wisdom of God surpasses all wisdom. His wisdom is mysterious, not even Satan can comprehend the wisdom of God. I wondered why five eggs were not sufficient for the doctors to bring about only one pregnancy. My God does not need more than one egg to produce a baby. Even twins are conceivable from only one egg. God is the greatest gynaecologist and obstetrician!

If you have been written off completely by the doctors and you feel let down or discouraged, I want to say to you that this is a golden opportunity for God to glorify Himself in your life. God cannot lie because He is not a man; He will bring His promise to pass in your life.

God is not a man, that he should lie, nor a son of man, that he should change his mind. Does he speak and then not act? Does he promise and not fulfill? (Numbers 23:19).

Faith and knowledge resting on the hope of eternal life, which God, who does not lie, promised before the beginning of time, and at his appointed season he brought his word to light through the preaching entrusted to me by the command of God our Savior (Titus 1:2,3).

CHAPTER 10

Only Christ Can Comfort You

I needed to be comforted frequently. But who can I go to every time without wearing the person out with my tears? It was as if I did not have the strength to go through another day without a solution. It was as if heaven was silent and shut against me.

Only Christ can comfort you. The most difficult period to praise the Lord is when you are in trouble and everything is against you.

During the time that I was waiting on the Lord, there were times I would freely worship the Lord and there were times I would find it difficult to talk to Him let alone sing His praises. But it got to a stage that I found it relieving to go before Him in songs. I would worship Him from the depths of my heart. I preferred to do my crying in His presence. Whenever I was upset with the situation, I would enter into a session of worship in my closet. At the end of the session, I always came out with floods of joy in my heart. Without the privilege of praise and worship, I do not know how I could have sailed through my season of barrenness.

I made up my mind not to cry in front of any man because I knew they would only pity me and think of ways to help me. There is nothing wrong in receiving words of comfort through other believers. In my experience, I realised that the true source of comfort is Christ and I was eager to tap into the Source.

The only instance where comfort from others could be harmful is when they start giving you ungodly counsel. I used to cry like a baby before my husband and he would try to comfort me but his words of comfort could not touch the depths of my aches. Once I discovered the comfort of being in the presence of God, I could no more settle for anything less.

Where else can one find comfort in this puzzling situation if not from the Father of all mercies and God of all comfort?

Praise be to the God and Father of our Lord Jesus Christ, the Father of compassion and the God of all comfort, who comforts us in all our troubles, so that we can comfort those in any trouble with the comfort we ourselves have received from God. For just as the sufferings of Christ flow over into our lives, so also through Christ our comfort overflows (II Corinthians 1:3-5).

He brings comfort to us in everything we go through. The Bible tells why He comforts us; He wants us to comfort those who suffer similar predicaments. If you have not received true comfort from God, how would you comfort someone else? What you do not have, you can not give. What you have not experienced you can not adequately share with others.

THE GREATEST COMFORT

It is important you receive comfort from God during your time of waiting. The following are hints on how to receive comfort from God in times of despair.

1. Go before the Lord in worship

Whenever the day came for Elkanah to sacrifice, he would give portions of the meat to his wife Peninnah and to all her sons and daughters. But to Hannah he gave a double portion because he loved her, and the LORD had closed her womb. And because the LORD had closed her womb, her rival kept provoking her in order to irritate her. This went on year after year. Whenever Hannah went up to the house of the LORD, her rival provoked her till she wept and would not eat. Elkanah her husband would say to her, "Hannah, why are you weeping? Why don't you eat? Why are you downhearted? Don't I mean more to you than ten sons?" Once when they had finished eating and drinking in Shiloh, Hannah stood up. Now Eli the priest

was sitting on a chair by the doorpost of the LORD's temple. In bitterness of soul Hannah wept much and prayed to the LORD. And she made a vow, saying, "O LORD Almighty, if you will only look upon your servant's misery and remember me, and not forget your servant but give her a son, then I will give him to the LORD for all the days of his life, and no razor will ever be used on his head." As she kept on praying to the LORD, Eli observed her mouth. Hannah was praying in her heart, and her lips were moving but her voice was not heard. Eli thought she was drunk and said to her, "How long will you keep on getting drunk? Get rid of your wine." "Not so, my lord," Hannah replied, "I am a woman who is deeply troubled. I have not been drinking wine or beer; I was pouring out my soul to the LORD. Do not take your servant for a wicked woman; I have been praying here out of my great anguish and grief." Eli answered, "Go in peace, and may the God of Israel grant you what you have asked of him." She said, "May your servant find favor in your eyes." Then she went her way and ate something, and her face was no longer downcast. Early the next morning they arose and worshiped before the LORD and then went back to their home at Ramah. Elkanah lay with Hannah his wife, and the LORD remembered her (1 Samuel 1:4-19).

2. Read God's word

I, even I, am he who comforts you. Who are you that you fear mortal men, the sons of men, who are but grass, that you forget the LORD your Maker,

> who stretched out the heavens and laid the foundations of the earth, that you live in constant terror every day because of the wrath of the oppressor, who is bent on destruction? For where is the wrath of the oppressor? (Isaiah 51:12,13).

> As a mother comforts her child, so will I comfort you; and you will be comforted over Jerusalem (Isaiah 66:13).

3. God can and will comfort you through other believers

> Who comforts us in all our troubles, so that we can comfort those in any trouble with the comfort we ourselves have received from God (II Corinthians 1:4b).

Hannah with a sorrowful spirit poured out her soul before the Lord. Through Eli God spoke words of reassurance and comfort to her and she left the place of prayer with joy. Whoever goes to God sorrowful never comes back the same.

Note that Elkanah (her husband) had tried to comfort her but his comfort did not relieve her agony. She went to God and something spectacular happened in her life as a result. The Lord remembered Hannah and she conceived in the course of time. You cannot make conception take place. There is time for everything under heaven and a time assigned to everyone to be born said King Solomon in

Ecclestiastes 2:3. Your time to bring a child to life will never pass you by in Jesus' name.

> **Early the next morning they arose and worshipped before the LORD and then went back to their home at Ramah. Elkanah lay with Hannah his wife, and the LORD remembered her. So in the course of time Hannah conceived and gave birth to a son. She named him Samuel, saying, "Because I asked the LORD for him (I Samuel 1:19,20).**

My prayer is that God will grant you the desire, courage and motivation to always come before Him with whatever problem you might be facing. He will also be merciful to you, as He is the Father of mercies and comfort. I pray that He will also flood your hearts with joy that knows no bound. No matter how difficult your situation is, your trust should always be in Him who is able to fulfil the desires of your heart. As He remembered Hannah, so will He remember you. As the bible records that in the course of time Hannah conceived so will your turn come in Jesus name. Amen.

CHAPTER 11

Remember Me, Oh Lord!

After a year of trying to conceive, I started to buy my baby things in faith. I even bought the clothes that my husband and I would wear for the christening. I was so sure that nothing could stop me from having children even though I did not know when this would happen.

PLEASE HIM WITH YOUR FAITH
Now faith is being sure of what we hope for and certain of what we do not see. This is what the ancients were commended for (Hebrews 11:1,2).

If you read this passage of Hebrews in its entirety you will discover that the men of old were commended for their faith. People like Abel, Enoch, Noah and Abraham the father of faith, to mention a few, obtained good testimonies through faith.

Your prayer will have to take a new dimension at this stage. It will no longer be a prayer of "please God, give me a child," it will now be a prayer of confessing and professing what the Lord has said about the situation. In line with what you believe and confess, you will start acting in faith.

And without faith it is impossible to please God, because anyone who comes to him must believe that he exists and that he rewards those who earnestly seek him (Hebrews 11:6).

The Lord opened my eyes to notice a trend to how He had been blessing people with children within the church. I sensed it in my spirit that He had been taking it in turn, so my prayer changed. I began to pray that my turn would come. He had promised me that He will bless me with children but I did not know when. I began to ask Him to *remember me*, and remind Him of the steps of faith I had taken in buying baby things according to the words He had spoken to me personally.

COVENANT-MAKING GOD

Early in 1996 the Lord told me to bring out all the things that I had bought so that He could see them. He then said I should present them to Him during my morning prayers for the first twelve days of the year. I did not know what this signified neither did it make any sense to me. But I had learnt to obey Him in the course of time regardless of whether He is making any sense or not to me—as long as I am convinced in my spirit that it is the Lord speaking to me. He is wiser than I am in every way.

For the foolishness of God is wiser than man's wisdom, and the weakness of God is stronger than man's strength (1 Corinthians 1:25).

I began to show these things to God during my morning prayers for the first twelve days of the year as He commanded. I will confess that I said these prayers after my husband had left for work. I could not tell him about it.

God is a covenant-making God. I believe that during this period He re-established His covenant with me that I will not be childless. I expected to conceive during that month but I did not. I felt disappointed and I purposed in my heart that if by the same time next year nothing happened, I would start giving out the baby things I had bought.

I had earlier discussed the IVF treatment we received (chapter 9). I will now discuss the bits that I left out because they are relevant to this chapter.

Before setting out to start the treatment, I went with my husband to one of my church pastors for prayer. The reason why we went for prayer then was to ask God's favour upon us as we went for the treatment so that it would be successful. We knew that I would take several medication that can tamper or alter the normal functioning of the body and did not want anything to go wrong in my body.

When my husband and I got to him we began to discuss about life generally. By the power of the Holy Spirit, he began to ask me questions that seemed irrelevant to my problems. He asked whether I have had a close friend in the past. He asked me about the friend and all that happened in our friendship.

Who has never had a close friend at a stage in their lives?, I said to myself, *and why should having a friend create a story? Why would a man of God want to know about such things?* As all these questions kept running through my mind, I replied "yes, I had a friend but we are no longer relating." He then said to me, "that's the more reason why you should tell me about this *close* friend of yours". He wanted to know why and how the relationship ended. (I will tell you about this friend in the next chapter).

Following my discussion with the man of God, deep things were uncovered by the power of the Holy Spirit. He then prayed with my husband and I. A word of prophecy also came through him that in a few weeks, I would conceive.

Immediately I heard this prophecy, doubts arose in my mind. *He had not prayed for more than ten minutes; we did not even talk about pregnancy and now he is prophesying that I will be pregnant in a few weeks time. Didn't he know that this problem of barrenness had been with me for a long time? Did he expect it to go away with less than ten minutes prayer?* These were my thoughts.

This unbelief of mine stemmed from the fact that I had been prayed for by several men of God. Some even prophesied that I would conceive the very month they prayed. My hopes had been raised several times only to come crashing down after the predicted time passed without conception. I did not want to be disappointed again.

What I learnt from this experience was the need to be aware of the wiles of the devil. If doubt is allowed to take root in the heart, one might miss God's visitation. Faith in God has to be consistent. It is not something that we practise today and abandon the next day. As you have read, you can deduce that I had my ups and downs with standing firm in faith. It is only God that can help you to stand firm without wavering.

Let us hold unswervingly to the hope we profess, for he who promised is faithful (Hebrews 10:23).

Each time my husband and I prayed, he would always stand on that prophecy, that in a few weeks I would be pregnant. Four months after this prophecy we were still praying "in a few weeks time." One day I said to my husband, "its four months now, how could you still be saying, in a few weeks time?" Maybe we should start saying in a few months time. But thank God for husbands who have faith! His answer to me was that "few weeks" would still be "few weeks" to him as long as it is under a year. So I had to comply with this routine daily prayer of "in a few weeks time...."

CHAPTER 12

How Could This Be?

In this chapter, I will discuss the relationship I had with someone I regarded as a close friend. She was the person the man of God who prayed with me in the previous chapter asked about. Let's call her name Aota.

I met Aota as a teenager in the hostel on my first day in college (in Nigeria). The moment we met, she was attracted to me and asked to be my friend. It seemed strange that someone would ask to be my friend on our very first meeting. I did not take her serious and thought it was just the common type of friendship that students make among themselves. She was a stranger and I was reluctant to associate with her.

We moved into the same block where she insisted that we should keep our foodstuffs in the same cupboard even though we were allocated separate rooms. Not wanting this, I kept my things in my own cupboard. However, whenever she wanted anything, she would come to my room and take it from my cupboard with the hope that I will go to her room when my provisions were exhausted. She was surprised that I did not come to her when we finished my provisions.

Before I continue with the story, I must say that the relationship was not sexual, however, it came to a stage when she started sleeping in my room. We would sleep together in the same single size bed. She so much wanted to be my only friend and for me to be hers. She did not allow anyone else to interact with me too closely. I could not have a stable male relationship during this period because she would always cause a split between us. She succeeded in this several times.

Whenever we had a disagreement, whoever tried to move closer to me among our mates was in big trouble. She would report to the lecturers that they were trying to take her friend away. Everyone in the college knew us.

At a stage in my course, we all had to move to a new hostel, and this time, we were allocated the same room. There were double bunk beds in these rooms. I took the top bed and she took the lower one. What surprised me was that she still would not sleep on her bed. We would either sleep in her bed or mine.

After a while, I noticed that things were missing from my wardrobe. I would look for my underwear, for instance, and not find it. Then after three months or so, I would find it at the same spot I had checked several times before. Being unsuspicious, I would wear these things again. I never thought of asking questions neither did I think it could be dangerous to wear them again. What mattered most to me was that they were in good condition and I had found them among my things.

After leaving college, we started looking for jobs. She insisted that we must look for jobs at the same place and if were unsuccessful, whoever got the job will not take it. We applied for jobs together and often made it known to the employer at the interview that we would prefer to work together.

Eventually, we got what we wanted. (Of course, she wanted to complete what she started in my life.) Unfortunately for her, the job was not going on well and we decided to resign. This time, she suggested that we leave separately. She suggested that I should leave first while she would stay to collect our salaries before joining me at the new place. What a good way to dispose of me! She seemed to have completed the most important aspect of her assignment.

What amazed me most was that during our time together, I never had a will of my own. Whatever she told me to do, I could not refuse. I always had to go by whatever she said.

She never joined me as she promised but occasionally would visit. During one of these visits, she took one of my dresses without telling me. I did not know about the missing dress until God revealed it to me in a dream after my conversion.

Some days later when Aota came to my house, I asked her to return my dress that she had taken but she denied taking it. Unannounced, I visited her place only to find that she actually had my clothe in her wardrobe! She had even taken a photograph with it! I inquired how she got it and why she denied taking it but she excused herself by saying, "because we no longer live together she still wants my smell around her." She confirmed that she took it during one of her visits to my place. This lady must have had such a great love for me!

After this episode, I began to see Aota in my dreams. She would ask me to follow her to a place. While on the way she would turn into a beast. I can still remember vividly how I would run back home in my dreams. This happened about three times. In other dreams, she would invite me to join her group. She always told me that if I joined them I would never be poor again. On every occasion, I refused.

In real life, she began to entice me with material things. She would buy me underwear, earrings, dresses, foodstuff and many other items. My mum wondered and asked me several times where she got the money from. I always answered, "she's got a good job and is well paid." Nonetheless, I kept asking myself, *was she working for me or for herself?* In addition to buying me things she would also give me money. *Um, what a caring friend she was*, I always pondered.

How Could This Be?

The Lord showed me a vision when we were both working in different towns. I was not even born again then. I saw that somebody would bring me a gift but I was warned not to open it. To my surprise, the following day, I received a well-wrapped gift from her. I remembered the vision and did not open it. Instead, I put it aside hoping to throw it away when I came back from work the following morning.

Unfortunately, my sister came back from work before me, saw the gift and opened it. That same week, she fell into a long, life-threatening illness which no doctor could name or find the cause. She was transferred from one hospital to the other yet nothing was detected during the investigations.

Eventually, we had to take her home, as she was near the point of death. It was the mercy of God and my family's prayers that saved her life. A prophecy came at the time that her illness came through a friend of "her sister".

I thank God that my sister was delivered and she is now well. What would have happened to me had I opened the gift? Apparently, Aota was trying to get back at me simply because I refused her invitation to join her group. God did not allow her to touch my life, although He allowed her to do several other things to me. I also believe God had ordained that I would not be a part of her occultic group.

At this point, I remembered Job. God allowed Job to suffer so much loss from the hand of the devil. However, the Lord warned Satan

.... but on the man himself do not lay a finger (Job 1:12).

God has a plan and purpose for my life so He protected me from the hands of the evil one. It was His power that prevented me from consenting to be a part of Aota's group.

Having seen all that happened to my sister I began to view Aota in a different light. I concluded that she was not an ordinary person, and I became afraid of her. My mum, brothers and sisters protested sternly that they did not want to see her in our house any longer. Whenever I saw her coming, I would run and hide from her.

One day, I summoned the courage to stand up to her but all I could say was that I wanted her to bring back the dress that she took from my wardrobe. Ironically, the dress was given to me by my sister who became ill. I insisted on taking back the dress despite all her excuses.

Very late one night, Aota turned up at my house after four months of staying away. She looked very sad with her eyes red. She stood at the door and threw in my missing cloth and ran away. We met at a friend's house once after this incident but never spoke to each other.

All this time, I was not a believer, very young without any knowledge of how to deal with such a situation. All the visions that the Lord gave to me during this time came by His grace and mercy. He was my refuge.

> **The LORD is a refuge for the oppressed, a stronghold in times of trouble (Psalm 9:9).**

CHAPTER 13

My Deliverance from "Aota" Spirit

Sometime after I became born again, I watched a screenplay by *Mount Zion Ministries*, a Christian organisation that ministers through drama presentations. After watching the play, I knew my friendship with Aota was not as ordinary as I had thought. From the sketch, I deduced that a lot of spiritual things had gone through the relationship and it had a demonic influence. I could sense that she had tampered with some things in my life but I could not pin down anything.

After watching the play, I prayed for myself and nullified any spiritual influence she had over me. I cast out any spirit she might have transferred in the course of our interactions. I never realised that the situation was not dealt with well enough. After my prayer, I forgot about everything altogether.

Aota never came to mind again until I went for prayer with the man of God that I had mentioned earlier on (chapter 11). After giving the man of God a detailed story about my friendship with Aota, he analysed the situation.

THE ANALYSIS

Aota had taken me to the spiritual realm for us to be married. She was my 'spiritual husband' and that was the reason why she cared so much for me. Her care for me manifested in the money and things I was given in the physical realm. She was always jealous whenever somebody else tried to get close to me or befriend me. This was because I was her wife in the spiritual realm which I knew nothing about.

The man of God also said that this union was done outside my will. I did not consent to joining her coven in the spiritual realm. Through a spirit of witchcraft, I was spiritually bonded to her against my will. I recalled seeing myself walking down an aisle as if getting married, but with no-one beside me.

Also, because she was a man in the spirit realm, it would be difficult for her to bear children in the physical. So she had to transfer to me all that belonged to her in exchange for what belonged to me. This was the reason why it was difficult for me to conceive when I became ready for it. I then saw the reason why the IVF treatment could not have solved my problem.

> **Can plunder be taken from warriors, or captives rescued from the fierce? But this is what the LORD says: "Yes, captives will be taken from warriors, and plunder retrieved from the fierce; I will contend with those who contend with you, and your children I will save (Isaiah 49:24,25).**

This analysis came as a shock and I found it difficult to believe initially. I basically could not bring myself to accept that she had done that much in my life without my knowledge.

The man of God pondered and asked a question after I narrated the story to him saying, "One thing I still don't understand is why did Aota pick you?" He could not give a reason and neither could I.

One thing I now know is that the hand of the Lord is upon my life. What happened between this girl and I was ordained for the name of the Lord to be glorified. Secondly, it was a kind of preparation for me. Everything was part of God's plan to prepare me for greater works—the good work God had ordained before the foundations of the earth (Ephesians 2:10).

The day after praying with the man of God, I had a dream. I saw Aota loading a vehicle. I asked her what she wanted from me again. She then responded that she had come to pack her belongings. At this I said to her, "pack your belongings and leave me in peace." When I woke up from the dream, I almost ran out of the flat!

The second day in January 1997, I saw Aota in my dreams again. I again asked her, "what else do you want from me"? She said that she had come to pack the rest of her things. She did so and left. I noticed that I conceived the very week that she packed the rest of her things.

CHAPTER 14

Spiritual Husbandry

Though many may find it hard to believe, spiritual husbandry is one of the main spiritual causes of infertility in women. Sadly, we no longer pay attention to this concept neither do we accept its authenticity. Could this be due to civilisation? The Bible teaches that we should not be ignorant of the devices of the enemy. There is no amount of technology or modernisation that can stop the devil from striking.

Spiritual husbandry is one of the ways the enemy is holding back children from people. Of course, if you still go to the hospital the doctors will find a name for the cause of infertility. The root of the problem may reveal illegal unions in the spiritual realm. Ignorance is one of the strongest weapons that the enemy is still using to prevent people's blessings from coming through.

SYMPTOMS

The following are some symptoms that can reveal a union in the realm of the spirit.

- Having sexual intercourse in your dreams.
- Having children in your dreams (there are exceptions, though).
- Getting married especially to someone you do not know in your dream.
- Dislike for your real husband.
- Lack of interest in having sex with your real husband. (All other reasons such as tiredness excluded).
- If your husband starts to regress after getting married to you; if he stops making progress in life.
- Menstruating in your dreams.
- And many more.

THEIR OPERATIONS

Spiritual husbands can do the following to a person's life.

- They can prevent a woman from getting married. The woman may be pretty inwardly and outwardly but still not find a suitable partner.

- They may prevent married women from having children.
- They may cause problems in marital relationships, problems like no affection for husband; poor sexual intimacy etc.
- They may prevent the spouse from making progress in life.

HANDLING SPIRITUAL HUSBANDS

You must realise that the enemy has been able to gain entry into your life through an *open door* made either knowingly or unknowingly. Hence, they have a legal ground to stand.

Doorways could be through past or present sins, generational sins, involvement in the occult and white garment churches, bitterness and unforgiveness. You will need to confess these sins and those of your generations past; ask God for forgiveness and never go back to them again.

If "spiritual husbands" have had *sexual relationship* with you in your dreams, ask God to clean you of the defilement, for your body is the temple of God.

If you are born again, you need to *nullify the covenant* that you have made with the spiritual husband in the name of Jesus Christ. Tell to him/her that the relationship between both of you has ceased. There is no other binding covenant apart from the one you have made with Jesus Christ and your real husband.

Begin to *confess* that your marriage to your real husband is the only authentic one. Mention your husband's name in prayer and affirm your relationship before God. Spiritual husbands are very stubborn so you might need to confess these several times in a day until there is total breakthrough.

You also need to *command* everything that was released into your body during sex to be without effect and to be removed.

Pray that God will arm you with strength and grace to resist having sex with them in your sleep. You may need to seek help from your pastor in this regard.

If you are not born again, you do not have any authority over the spiritual husband. You need to follow the steps in chapter two and give your life to Christ. After you are born again, you can proceed with the steps given on this chapter to rebuke the spiritual husband.

CHAPTER 15

Break The Legal Ground of Curses

A curse is one of the hidden sources of barrenness. The curse could be a result of disobedience to God's word. It could also be a result of handling accursed things, in which case the devil has a legal ground in one's life. Satan or other people without any just reason, could also place curses on someone. The most dangerous curse that people carry about unknowingly is the one that is self-pronounced.

Before I go ahead in this chapter, I shall define what I mean by curses. According to the *Oxford Popular Dictionary*, a curse is *a call for evil to come on a person or thing; a great evil or violent exclamation of anger; afflict.*

The medium through which curses are pronounced and carried out are demonic spirits. I remember the dream I had when I started waiting on God for the fruit of the womb. A demon spirit confronted me saying I would not be able to get pregnant and that she was the demon spirit assigned to ensure this. I was still young in the Lord and did not know anything about curses. So, I took the dream very lightly.

From what I now know, there was a curse upon my life. It could have been from one or several of the sources which I have discussed in this book, including, disobedience to God, evil pronouncement from false prophets, involvement with white garment (occult) churches, handling cursed and unholy things. I would now discuss two other possible curses that can hinder your quest for a child and how they can be dealt with.

GENERATIONAL CURSE

Your ancestors might have traded a family blessing for power or wealth or any other desire of theirs. They might have also lived a ruthless life and someone more powerful and evil could have placed a curse upon the family. Such generational curses can affect up to the four generations (Exodus 20:5).

Broken agreements with Satan (which happens often when you accept Christ as your Lord and Saviour), may also bring a curse until they are dealt with. If you were not dedicated to Jesus Christ when you were born, you must have been dedicated to something else (especially if you are of African origin). Any deviation from whatever you have been dedicated to will always cause a problem when you accept Christ because there was a break in a legal (and binding) contract, but God will see you through. This might also explain why people say (after accepting Christ as their Lord and Savior), that everything stopped going well for a while.

Curses can also come from your ancestors' worship of false gods. I was living under a generational curse but did not realise it. My maternal great grandfather was a very wicked hunter in his days. He wronged so many people. As a result a curse was placed upon every female in the family. The curse ensured that every daughter from his family will always have problems when they got married. I knew about the curse before I got married but did not think I could be affected in any way. I reasoned that I did not know the man neither was I the one who did the wrong. But the hard and bitter truth of it all is that I did not have to know him neither did I have to have commit the wrong. The most important thing is that a family line had been cursed and without rectification, it will have effect over the people it is aimed at.

When you observe the same kind of problem running in a family, the symptom might prove to be a hereditary disease, that is, a disease that is inherited from the family. For example, a mother may have had fertility problems and all her daughters are having fertility problems or the same disease that caused infertility.

To undo this kind of curse, you need to acknowledge the sin of your forefathers or ancestors. Ask God to forgive you and your ancestors, then renounce the curse aloud in the name of Jesus Christ. We have all authority in Jesus Christ.

SELF-PRONOUNCED CURSES

Self-pronounced curses can easily go undetected although one will continue to suffer for the self-inflictions. There are so many things that people utter against themselves unknowingly. Some women are used to calling their menstrual period a "curse." Some women have rejected the idea of childbearing when they were younger simply because they were not ready for it at the time, not realising that every word uttered has implications. Life and death is in the power of the tongue (Proverbs 18:21).

I said many negative words several times before I got married. I was completely unaware of their effect until I read a book written by Derek Prince titled *Blessing or Curses* (highly recommended).

You can renounce these curses yourself by speaking out loud and rejecting them. But first, you need to ask God to forgive you for uttering such things with your mouth. Do not forget that we will all give account of every idle word that we speak.

CHAPTER 16

And The Lord Remembered Me!

During the first week in January of 1997, my husband and I decided to declare the new year as a year of *affirmation, attestation* and *acknowledgement* of the word of God. This meant we would be affirming, confirming, confessing and attesting to what God had said about us. We searched for scriptures in line with our situation. These scriptures we affirmed morning, afternoon and night.

GOD BROKE MY FAST!

I began a 40-day daily fast, eager that nothing would stop me from completing it. I became unwell ten days into the fast. So, I continued to bind the devil, telling him that he would not stop me from completing the fast.

Eventually, God spoke to me through another dream. In the dream, I was holding a hungry baby. When I woke up, I knew God was trying to tell me something. Because of how I was feeling and the dream I had, I decided to undertake a pregnancy test. I had done several tests in the past. Knowing how disappointing it could be if the result was negative, I was not too eager.

Despite this, I went to the chemist and bought a kit. It would normally take me thirty minutes to get home from the chemist. I thought half an hour was too long to discover what lied ahead. So, I went into a public toilet to carry out the test. I guessed what the result would be but at the same time I was nervous in case it was not what I thought.

THE JOYOUS TURNAROUND

My vision became blurred with tears as I waited for the result. When I was able to see properly, I saw that the result was positive. Immediately, the tears of fear and uncertainty, tears of an inward plea for a turnaround in my situation, turned into tears of joy and thanksgiving! Within a twinkle of an eye, I stepped out of infertility to fertility; from aspiring mother to expectant mother! I could not contain the joy that filled my entire body. I almost stopped the person that I met on leaving the toilet to tell her that I was expecting a baby! I went to my husband's office straightaway to tell him about the good news - *the gospel according to our first baby!*

When I told him about it, I expected him to jump up and shout for joy. But you know what? He just said, "thank God" and expressed no emotion. I was very surprised. He then told me that he had never thought that we would not have children. He knew that the child will come in God's own time.

RESISTING DISCOURAGEMENT

About a week after our discovery, I went to see our new family doctor to inform him that I was pregnant but he tried to dampen my joy. He told me that even if I carried the pregnancy test out one hundred times and they were all positive he would not be moved by it. As far as he was concerned, the first investigations carried out revealed that I could not get pregnant, and he was not expecting anything contrary to these results. Even when the second investigation revealed that my reproductive organs were in good condition, he did not acknowledge it. He told me to go home and expect my period to come and that I was just experiencing a delay which is very common.

Upon hearing what he had to say, I jumped out of my seat and began to audibly rebuke the devil speaking through him. Right in front of him, I rejected all the negative things he had said in Jesus' name! (Never be ashamed to stand for what you believe and the word of God concerning your situation). I also told him that I was pregnant. "I will not menstruate for the next nine months, not because of any disease but because I am pregnant." He was startled, quiet and stood amazed as I left the clinic.

The following week, I went back to him to ask for a referral to the Hospital's Ante-natal clinic but he refused. He insisted on a hospital pregnancy test at six weeks. So, I had to go back home and wait until I was six weeks pregnant. The devil always try to steal your joy when God gives you a breakthrough. Never allow him. For about three weeks after the first pregnancy test that I did privately, the devil tried to suppress my joy but I prevailed over him.

The test was eventually carried out. I had to wait another week for the result. Waiting at this stage was a bit difficult but God helped me. When I called him on the phone to get the result, I felt the reluctance in his voice. He just said casually, "it is positive, bye," and he dropped the handset.

PRECIOUS EXPERIENCES

I became even more joyful as the days rolled into weeks and weeks into months. I passionately expected the early symptoms of pregnancy. It was an amazing experience to watch my body change from the skinny, flat-tummy shape into a plumy, big-bellied expectant mother! I cannot overemphasise the tremendous change in my eating habit from the second trimester (4-6 months). I began to appreciate food, especially food that I never ate when I was not pregnant.

Knowing that I was carrying a baby in my tummy was something that I could not explain or comprehend. Watching the baby during my first scan totally confounded me. The memory of the first scan will forever remain with me. It was amazing to see the baby for the first time through the screens. It was wonderful to know what God can do in someone's life when He is ready to move. I began to see God from a new perspective. He is indeed an awesome God. It was wonderful to see the baby moving his tiny limbs in the fluid. Medical scientists will call him an embryo or foetus, but we called him baby right from the onset. Indeed the Lord saw our substance when we were yet unformed; He formed the raw materials that we were made of. He skilfully knit us in our mothers womb. Amazing!

I must testify that I enjoyed the period of pregnancy. I derived so much joy in buying my baby's things and preparing for him. Even though I was a qualified midwife and had helped deliver several babies in the past, I had not paused to think of how awesome my God is until I personally experienced delivery. My labour and delivery was normal and our baby weighed 4.04kg.

I passed from being an expectant mother to being a mum! Words cannot describe the joy of holding your own baby. The joy was overwhelming that I could not sleep the first night, not because the baby disturbed me but because I just could not keep my eyes off the tiny little creature! I then understood that God wanted Abraham and Sarah to derive pleasure and satisfaction from holding Isaac when He insisted that the child of promise will come out of their bodies, not from Hagar (which would have been surrogacy), or Eliezer of Damascus (which would have been adoption).

As I gazed at our baby, I smiled because I knew that the battle of childlessness was over. If there was any other battle I had to fight (and I was aware the war was still on), it would not be over conception and pregnancy. Through Christ, I was more than a conqueror in that arena. To Him be all the glory!

MY PRAYER FOR YOU

God will take you from a level of being an aspiring mother to becoming an expectant mother and ultimately becoming a joyful mother of children. As the Bible recalled that Elizabeth gave birth at full term, so will you. You will not miscarry your pregnancy. You will enjoy the period of pregnancy, labour, delivery and motherhood.

As God turned on the waters to destroy the earth, He made a promise to Noah that he and his family with the animals that were with him would not be destroyed; as He remembered and kept His promises regarding the animals in the ark, so will God remember and keep His promises concerning you. He will hold you by the hand and lead you out of the raging waters of childlessness.

The week I conceived was exactly a year after the covenant the Lord had made with me — when He told me to bring out, for the first twelve days of that year,

And the Lord Remembered Me!

all the baby things that I had bought . God honoured His word and remembered me. He also honoured the prophecy of the man of God, the continual prayer of my husband, and my obedience to His instruction. The Lord will honour you also with the desire of your heart.

CHAPTER 17

He Is Never Too Late

You have prayed, confessed sins, rejected negative pronouncements, confessed positive words, fasted and even undergone prayer of deliverance but nothing has happened. You feel discouraged because it seems God does not care about you and all that you are going through. You feel as if God has not been faithful to His promises. I want you to know that feelings are deceitful but the word of God is perfect and sure.

Has your condition worsened despite all your prayers? Is all hope lost? Maybe you are approaching or have even reached menopause. Have you been told that it is too late to rectify the condition? You might have been told that there is nothing else to do to help you. Well, I have good news for you. The God of Abraham, the God of Isaac and the God of Jacob specialises in rotten situations. A similar story is found in John 11:1-45. It is the story of Lazarus, Jesus' friend.

Why would Jesus allow His friend, Lazarus to die before visiting him? Mary, Lazarus' sister, sent a message to Jesus that His friend was ill. Jesus, knowing the end from the beginning, said *"this sickness is not unto death but for the glory of God..."* My prayer for you today is that no matter how damaged your reproductive organs are, God will make you whole again and He will be glorified in your situation. The disease that is affecting your reproductive organs will not bring death to the organs, rather it will bring glory to God. Why would God not give Sarah a baby until she was 90 years? What could He not do when she was younger that He did when she became 90 years?

JESUS LOVES YOU

Jesus did not visit Lazarus until four days after his death when his body had begun to rot. Even when He received Mary's message that Lazarus was not well, He stayed where He was for another two days. Does Jesus' attitude reflect love for Lazarus? Verse 3 of the text says, "...Lord, behold Lazarus whom you love is sick." This verse tells us that He loved Lazarus. Verse 5 confirms that He also loved Martha, Mary and Lazarus.

There are some situations that God will not attend to immediately after prayers are offered. No matter how fervent your prayers, God, at times, will allow some situations to rot before He lifts a finger. This does not mean God hates you neither does it mean

He is too late. He simply wants to glorify Himself through the situation. When He said the sickness will be to the glory of God, Jesus was not just wishing, He knew the end from the beginning.

At a point, I thought God hated me. This was during my first year of waiting. I thought God had favourites and I just was not one of them. However, He dealt with me so much on this issue that I began to see this as a lie of the devil. You may not fully understand why you are going through some things, but settle it in your mind that God loves you and He is never too late.

NOT MOVED BY ACCUSATIONS

Martha heard Jesus was coming and went to meet Him on the way. She did not challenge Him in front of the mourners. But, when she got to Him she accused Him, "Lord, if you had been here, my brother would not have died (verse 21)."

Are you accusing God, saying, "Lord if you had answered my prayers and cries all these days or years, my situation would not have worsened"? Mary made the same accusation against Christ (verse 32). God, however, does not respond to accusations.

MOVED BY WORDS OF FAITH

It was only after Martha spoke words of faith that Jesus responded. Martha said, "but even now I know that whatever you ask of God, God will give you." To this "Jesus said to her, your brother will rise again" (verse 23). As you make Martha's confession your own today, I pray that God in His mercy will speak His word to your body and any dead reproductive organ will rise again. The Lord will resurrect the dead areas of your organs in Jesus' name.

MOVED BY TEARS

Also, Jesus was not moved by Mary's accusation but by her weeping. The Bible says that when He saw them weeping He groaned in the spirit and was troubled. His groaning was not an ordinary one but an intercession on behalf of Lazarus and his sisters.

That He was troubled did not mean He was worried or anxious. It only revealed a burden in His heart for this particular problem. He proceeded to ask them where they had laid him.

The tears you have shed because of barrenness have not gone unnoticed; they will cause the Lord to be moved on your behalf and ask you, "daughter, where does the problem lie?"

> ... weeping may endure for the night but joy comes in the morning (Psalm 30:5b, NKJV).

I speak prophetically into your life: your morning has come. Henceforth, you will begin to experience true joy. The days of your weeping are ended.

MOVED WITH COMPASSION

The Lord was moved with compassion and wept because He felt what they were going through. You are not going through it alone; He is with you and can feel the pain, aches, sorrows and persecutions you are experiencing. He is with you all the way. Has He not said that He will never leave you nor forsake you? When the Israelites were passing through the Red Sea and the Jordan River, the Lord did not allow the waters to overwhelm them. He saw them through. In the same way, Shadrach, Meshach and Abednego were thrown into the fire, yet the flame did not scorch them because the Lord was with them.

> **When you pass through the waters, I will be with you; and when you pass through the rivers, they will not sweep over you. When you walk through the fire, you will not be burned; the flames will not set you ablaze. For I am the LORD, your God, the Holy One of Israel, your Savior; I give Egypt for your ransom, Cush and Seba in your stead. Since you are precious and honored in my sight, and because I love you, I will give men in exchange for you, and people in exchange for your life. Do not be afraid, for I am with you; I will bring your children from the east and gather you from the west. I will say to the north, `Give them up!' and to the south, `Do not hold them back.' Bring my sons from afar and my daughters from the ends of the earth — (Isaiah 43:2-6).**

JESUS OUR INTERCESSOR

Jesus again, moving towards His friend's tomb, groaned in His spirit. The fact that He has finished His earthly ministry does not mean that He cannot intercede on our behalf anymore. He is still our High Priest, Representative, Advocate and Intercessor.

> **... Christ Jesus, who died - more than that, who was raised to life - is at the right hand of God and is also interceding for us (Romans 8:34).**

"If I could hear Christ praying for me in the next room, I would not fear a million enemies, yet distance makes no difference He is praying for me" (Martin Luther).

TAKE AWAY THE STONE

"Take away the stone", he said. "But, Lord," said Martha, the sister of the dead man, "by this time there is a bad odor, for he has been there four days" (John 11:39).

Jesus commanded that the stone covering the tomb be taken away. The stone signifies anything that will prevent God from reaching out to you. Fear, anxiety, worry, doubt or unbelief will serve as a hindrance to receiving God's blessing. You have prayed and fasted but it seemed as if your prayers were bouncing back at you. You may be thinking that the problem has gone on for so long that it can no longer leave. You have accepted it as part of your lifestyle and have built your life round it. Does the problem seem as big and heavy as the stone that covered the tomb? You think there is no way for God to reach you. You think no one can help you. No matter what you think, the word of God to you is two-fold.

First, roll away the stone (John 11:39). Roll away the stone of despair, fear, anxiety, worry and unbelief. Be willing to seek help if you are unable to roll away the stone all by yourself.

The second word is,

"...if you would believe you would see the glory of God" (John 11:40).

Act on your belief by laying your problem before God. Do not hide it from Him. Do not pretend you are able to handle it on your own when you obviously need His help. It was when the stone of unbelief was rolled away that Jesus reached out to call Lazarus forth. As you roll away the stone of fear, doubt, anxiety and worry from your way, I pray that He will reach out to you and call your children forth into manifestation. As Lazarus was loosed from his grave clothes so will you be loosed from all the shackles of the enemy, in Jesus' name.

At the appointed time, Lazarus was brought back to life. There is time for everything and our God is never late. He is always on time. Whatever happens during the waiting period will be to His glory. So rest in Him.

CHAPTER 18

Abraham & Sarah

I learnt a lot from the life of Abraham and Sarah while I waited to get pregnant. I will share in this chapter some of the things I learnt from these patriarchs of faith about the problem of childlessness.

> After this, the word of the LORD came to Abram in a vision: 'Do not be afraid, Abram. I am your shield, your very great reward' But Abram said, "O Sovereign LORD, what can you give me since I remain childless and the one who will inherit my estate is Eliezer of Damascus?" And Abram said, "You have given me no children; so a servant in my household will be my heir." Then the word of the LORD came to him: "This man will not be your heir, but a son coming from your own body will be your heir." He took him outside and said, "Look up at the heavens and count the stars--if indeed you can count them." Then he said to him, "So shall your offspring be." Abram believed the LORD, and he credited it to him as righteousness (Genesis 15:1-6).

The Lord appeared to Abram in a vision, but when the He first spoke to him, he could not relate to what God had to say. They were just like ordinary words.

God said to Abram, "do not be afraid, Abram. I am your shield, your exceedingly great reward." The Lord knew about Abram's fears even without him saying a word and He ministered to him. He said, "do not be afraid." He even called Abram by name. Whatever your fears, God knows about them. He knows your concerns. He knows you by name.

He also said to him "I am your shield." According to the Oxford Popular Dictionary, a shield is *a piece of armour carried on the arm to protect the body*. This tells me that the Lord was always around Abraham to protect him. He is always with you to offer you protection in whatever you are going through.

He also made it known to him that He was his "exceedingly great reward;" not just a *rewarder*, but his *reward*. What more could anyone ask for? He is your reward.

In *verse* 2, Abram opened up to God. He realised that the Lord knew about his fears and concerns. Despite the word of the Lord that came to him, he still did not acknowledge or thank God for His promises. All he could see was his childlessness. He focused on his present state. The NKJV puts verse 2 this way, "but Abram said, 'Lord God, what will you give me, *seeing* I go childless, and the heir of my house is Eliezer of Damascus?" He could not see beyond his present state.

For you to be able to move fully into the promise and purpose of God for your life you will need to see beyond your present circumstance. Begin to see what God is seeing concerning your life.

In *verse 3*, I believe God must have asked Abram a question following what he asked God in verse 2. The question could have been, "Abram, what made you think you will go childless? What made you think Eliezer your servant will be your heir?" This must have generated Abram's response when he said, "look, you have given me no offspring; indeed one born in my house is my heir!" (NKJV). Still he could only see what was around him. He told God to "look" at his situation.

What can you see in your present state? *What made you think that you will go childless? What made you think that you can only adopt or go through surrogacy?*

The word of the Lord came to him again, "this one shall not be your heir, but one who will come from your own body shall be your heir." The Lord made it known to Abram that he would not have to adopt before the promise is fulfilled. "Oh, Abram, your heir will come from your own body not from somebody else's. Not by surrogacy; not by adoption. Stand firm on My word. Let My word become real to you."

The word and the promises of God concerning your children need to become real to you. Begin to see children around you. See yourself feed and care for your children. Stand firm on the word of God. The bible says,

**...and having done all, to stand. Stand therefore...
(Ephesians 6:13-14, NKJV).**

In *verse 5*, God brought Abram outside and said, "look now towards heaven, ...and so shall your descendants be." In other words, God was saying, "Abram, now that you have My word in your spirit, look upwards; begin to see what I am seeing concerning your situation. You can now look and see me turn your impossibilities to possibilities." "Look now to heaven" where your help comes from; the throne of grace where you will find mercy to help in your situation.

Verse 6 says, "and Abram believed in the Lord..." This happened when his spiritual eyes opened. May the Lord help you to begin to see what He is seeing regarding your situation. He will also help your faith to rise.

Zechariah, the father of John the Baptist, became mute because he did not believe in the good tidings brought by the angel. He could not speak until his child had been named. Perhaps the Lord closed his mouth to keep him from confessing negative things which would have hindered what the Lord wanted to do in his life! God does not like it when we distrust Him or His word. When we do not believe in His word we make Him a liar.

And the angel answered and said to him, "I am Gabriel, who stands in the presence of God, and

was sent to speak to you and bring you these glad tidings. "But behold, you will be mute and not able to speak until the day these things take place, because you did not believe my words which will be fulfilled in their own time." (Luke 1:19,20).

Soon after the conversation between Abram and God, something unfortunate happened in Genesis 16:1-6,

Now Sarai, Abram's wife, had borne him no children. But she had an Egyptian maidservant named Hagar; so she said to Abram, "The LORD has kept me from having children. Go, sleep with my maidservant; perhaps I can build a family through her." Abram agreed to what Sarai said. So after Abram had been living in Canaan ten years, Sarai his wife took her Egyptian maidservant Hagar and gave her to her husband to be his wife. He slept with Hagar, and she conceived. When she knew she was pregnant, she began to despise her mistress. Then Sarai said to Abram, "You are responsible for the wrong I am suffering. I put my servant in your arms, and now that she knows she is pregnant, she despises me. May the LORD judge between you and me." "Your servant is in your hands," Abram said. "Do with her whatever you think best." Then Sarai mistreated Hagar; so she fled from her.

Sarah was worried that she may never be able to bear children. So, she said to Abraham, "see now that the Lord has restrained me from bearing children" (verse 2). She considered God as her enemy, and decided to tackle the problem in her own way. In verses 3 and 4, she offered her maidservant, Hagar, to her husband. It is a mistake to make decisions out of anxiety and fear. If you are not sure of what to do, wait until you have received clarity from God. It was lack of patience that drove me to IVF.

Soon after Hagar conceived, Sarah realised that she had made the biggest mistake of her life (verse 5). Considering the kind of reassurance that God gave Abram earlier on, who would have thought that he could easily succumb to such a suggestion from his wife?

OPEN UP TO GOD

When you are worried, anxious and fretful about your problems, who do you turn to for the restoration of your peace? Where do you go for comfort and reassurance? Abram, in his time of discouragement, worry and anxiety, opened up to the Lord. He carried all his cares to Him. The Bible says in Isaiah 66:13,

> As the one whom his mother comforts, so I will comfort you and you shall be comforted in Jerusalem (NKJV).

God knew that Abram was beginning to think of an adopted heir and the word of the Lord came to him regarding this. What God had in mind was different from what Abram was contemplating. The Lord had made it known to him that a child from his own body will be his heir. The Bible records in verse 6 that Abram believed in the Lord. The Bible says in Isaiah 55:8-9,

> **For My thoughts are not your thoughts, nor are your ways My ways says the Lord. For as the heavens are higher than the earth so are My ways higher than your ways and My thoughts than your thoughts (NKJV).**

He is the God of all mercy and comfort, who comforts us in all our tribulations (see 2 Corinthians 1:3-4). It is only Him who can help you find absolute peace in the midst of your troubles.

TAKE WISE COUNSEL

You need to be careful in taking other people's advice. Satan has not desisted from his deceitful schemes. Abram, having been told by God that his heir will come from his own body, still accepted Sarah's advice of going into Hagar. It seemed like what God wanted to use. Genesis 17:18, says

> **and Abraham said to the Lord, "Oh, that Ishmael might live before you" (NKJV).**

Ishmael looked like the real promise to him. In my own case, IVF looked like what God wanted to use. Actually, God had a different plan. I was clear what God had in mind. I knew it was a spiritual battle. He never said that I would conceive through IVF. You need to know exactly what God is saying about your situation and be able to recognise it when you see it. You need to follow your "Journey Planner" just as I shared earlier.

Be very vigilant. Your spouse might even be the person who would make the wrong suggestion. Opinions, things that seem like open doors, tend to come around the time you are to have your *real* breakthrough. If you make the mistake of falling into the trap, your testimony will be affected.

I was to start another IVF treatment a month before the time I conceived naturally. The only reason why I could not start the treatment was that I was on a six months in-service training. I thought if I should have the treatment while in training, it would be too strenuous for me and the treatment might fail again. I, therefore, decided to put the treatment aside until the end of the course. It was not that I loved the course more than having a baby but I believe God guided me into making the decision. Knowing how much I longed to have a baby, I would not have chosen the course over the treatment. I ought to have gone for the training six months earlier but for no obvious reason, I was refused a placement. The Bible says, and we know that all things work together for good to those who love God to those who are the called according to His purpose (Romans 8:28, NKJV).

THINK ABOUT THE FUTURE

Sarah decided to help herself when she became worried,

Now Sarai, Abram's wife, had borne him no children. But she had an Egyptian maidservant named Hagar; so she said to Abram, "The LORD has kept me from having children. Go, sleep with my maidservant; perhaps I can build a family through her." Abram agreed to what Sarai said (Genesis 16:1-2).

Sarah was worried that she could die childless. So, she gave Hagar to her husband and that became a problem not only to her, but also to Christians up till today. There will always be problems when you decide to do things your own way. You might step into problems that will have consequences for the rest of your life. Abraham sought God's counsel and he found peace but Sarah got into trouble because she tried to help herself.

SHARE WITH YOUR SPOUSE

Communication between couples matter a lot especially when there is a crisis in the home.

Abraham failed to relate God's promise of a heir to Sarah. As a priest in the house, husbands ought always to communicate what God has said regarding their situation. Satan used the gap in communication to cause further problems in Abraham's family.

Satan knows how to take advantage of an existing problem, so do not give him the chance. No matter how tough the situation may seem, even if it looks impossible, do not give in or settle for less.

> **I will bless her and will surely give you a son by her. I will bless her so that she will be the mother of nations; kings of peoples will come from her." Abraham fell facedown; he laughed and said to himself, "Will a son be born to a man a hundred years old? Will Sarah bear a child at the age of ninety?" And Abraham said to God, "If only Ishmael might live under your blessing!" Then God said, "Yes, but your wife Sarah will bear you a son, and you will call him Isaac. I will establish my covenant with him as an everlasting covenant for his descendants after him (Genesis 17:16-19).**

God reaffirmed His promise to Abraham. Note what Abraham's reply was, "...will a son be born to a man a hundred years old? Will Sarah bear a child at the age of ninety?" Yes, it looked impossible but the Bible says that,

> **...with God nothing shall be impossible, (Luke 1:37, NKJV).**

DON'T SETTLE FOR SECOND BEST

Then Abraham went further to say that Ishmael, the child born to him by Hagar was enough for him. It was like telling God, "don't worry anymore, we'll settle for Ishmael." Abraham was fed up with the problem. He had managed to get himself into a comfort zone, which he was not prepared change. He felt comfortable with Ishmael and wanted to put the problem of barrenness behind him when it was not yet over.

Well, God being God, would not let that happen. He made Abraham realise that He had not finished with him; the promised covenant child would come from Sarah and not Hagar. "I am the Lord who watches over My word to perform it, I have promised you and I will bring it to pass. I am the Boss here, you don't dictate to Me what to do." The Lord did not relent until He had brought it to pass.

THERE IS A SET TIME

There is a time for everything. God has set times for every plan He has for your life. God eventually revealed His set time to Abraham in Genesis 17:21,

But my covenant I will establish with Isaac, whom Sarah shall bear to you at this set time next year (NKJV).

And the Lord visited Sarah; she conceived and bore a child to Abraham in his old age at the set time which God had spoken to him.

> **Now the LORD was gracious to Sarah as He had said, and the LORD did for Sarah what he had promised. Sarah became pregnant and bore a son to Abraham in his old age, at the very time God had promised him (Genesis 21:1-2).**

When God is ready to move, there is nothing like "she is too old to conceive" or "she has reached menopause." There is nothing like "my husband's sperm count is too low" or "I am not ovulating." When He works, no one can stop Him. God's timing is very crucial. Getting us to wait till a certain period does not mean He has forsaken us. Delay is not denial. "Wait" does not mean "No." The time that God has purposed for you to have your child will not pass you by. The bible says in Ecclesiastes 3:1,

> ...that to everything there is a season, a time for every purpose under heaven (NKJV).

When we had our son, we realised that this was God's perfect time. We would not have been able to cope with bringing him up with the financial and physical responsibilities had he arrived earlier. The Lord had to prepare us for four years before He blessed us with a child.

CHAPTER 19

He Will Do It Again!

The purpose of this chapter is to encourage women experiencing secondary infertility and those filled with anxiety after a delayed and traumatic first experience.

After I had my first baby, I became concerned that I might not be able to give birth to another. I also thought that even if I was able to have more, it might take as long as the first one did or longer.

In addition, the Lord had asked me to write this book and I was concerned about what people would say if I had only one child—considering the fact that I would be writing on the issue of barrenness and childbearing. *People might think it was just a good fortune for me to have had a child.*

In view of this, I began to ask God for a second child. I was specific about the time I wanted to carry the pregnancy because I considered myself not ready at the time. Even though I knew that I would prefer to have another child *before* writing the book, and knowing the kind of urgency on God's heart concerning it, I still insisted on my own timing. Nevertheless, I began to write.

Halfway through, I stopped and started telling God all over again how I thought I should not write the book without having another child. At this stage the Lord became quiet and the inspiration ceased. I knew straightaway that I had grieved God's Spirit. So, I repented and continued writing even without a second child.

My concerns were ministered to during one of our church services through a song. The part of the song that released me from my fear is this:

You may not know how,
You may not know when,
But He will do it again.

I stood on these words that I will never know how the pregnancy will come, I would never know when it will happen but the Lord will do it again.

Two days after I completed writing the book, I began to feel unwell. I treated myself for hay fever but the symptom persisted. I repeated the treatment for several weeks without any improvement. I was on my way to the chemist to buy a stronger medication for this "stubborn fever" when the Lord told me to buy a pregnancy test kit. I remember saying to the Lord, "Father, this is hay fever, I had the same symptom last year. It just was not this bad."

On getting to the chemist, I thought I would buy the pregnancy kit and do the test just to fulfill all righteousness because I knew very well from my calculation that I could not be pregnant. The pharmacist insisted she would not sell the hay fever medication if I thought I was pregnant. I pleaded with her and convinced her I knew what I was doing.

The pain was getting unbearable and I wanted something to relieve it. I wanted to do the test quickly so I could take the medication.

As I was going into the bathroom, all sorts of thoughts began to run through my mind. *What if I was pregnant? What if I was not? But I ovulated just last week and I abstained from sex.* I kept thinking I could not be pregnant. I was nervous. My heart started pounding rapidly. My hands were shaking as I began to unwrap the pregnancy test kit. I had to wait for about two minutes before reading the result, but it seemed like two hours.

Finally, the result showed up on the panel. It was positive! I was pregnant again! The first question that I asked was, *how and when did I get pregnant? I should not be pregnant by my own calculations,* I kept wondering. The more I tried to figure out how it happened, the more confused I got. The Lord confounded me. Up till today, I still cannot figure out how and when the Lord did it. This reminds me of the words of the song that I stood on:

You may not know how,
You may not know when,
But He will do it again.

How and when did it happen? I still don't know. All that I know is that He has done it again!

Following this, I became worried that all the hay fever medication would have harmed my child. My husband and I prayed about it. I delivered a normal healthy baby girl at full term weighing 3.90kg.

If you have had a child before and want more but are finding it difficult, I want to encourage you that the Lord who did the previous one will do it again. You may not know how, you may not know when but the Lord will do it again. The Bible says in Psalm 113:9

He grants a barren woman a home, like a *joyful mother of children*.

He did not say joyful mother of *a child* but joyful mother of *children* – and that is what you are!

For more information about the author and
her ministry to women;
or for counselling and prayer support,
please write through the following:

Email
author@joyfulmothers.com
toyin@joyfulmothers.org

Website
www.joyfulmothers.org
www.joyfulmothers.com

If you have been blessed by reading this book and
have comments or testimonies, please write the
author using either of the email addresses above.
Thank You.

Watch out for more titles in the *Joyful Mother* series.

The *Emmanuel House* Vision:

Spreading the knowledge of God's glory
to the ends of the earth
by raising writers
and releasing classics;

Expounding the mind of God
for this present generation;

Motivating and inspiring
God's people towards
reality, purpose and destiny.